QUICK HIT
SALES T.I.P.S.

Tactics to Improve Professional Sellers

10 T.I.P.S. to help you outsell your competition,
maximize customer value, & win more deals, faster!

Scott Kaplan

Quick Hit Sales T.I.P.S.
—Tactics to Improve Professional Sellers

10 T.I.P.S. to help you outsell your competition, maximize customer value, and win more deals faster!

Published by JWC Publishing

JWC PUBLISHING
WHAT'S YOUR STORY?

ISBN: 979-8-9865278-1-9

Printed in the United States of America

What Others Are Saying

Scott's experience, tips, and tricks work. I've seen his approach improve sales rep results so they make more money. In turn, companies leveraging Scott's approach reduce ramp time while improving CAC. If you are a new rep, a 20-year veteran, or a Chief Revenue Officer – Scott's strategy and tactics are critical for you to master for continued sales success.

> –Paul Albright, Goldman Sachs Operating Partner and Technology Board member/CEO/CRO

As we continue to navigate an ever-changing sales landscape with new modes of communication, it's critical that we train sales professionals in an efficient and effective way. Scott is a one-of-a-kind expert who understands foundational sales truths while being able to leverage an efficient and easily understood sales training process. These quick hit sales tips will benefit your team and level up your ability to manage growing revenue demands.

> –Chris Sharpe
> Chief Revenue Officer at SubSplash

If sellers take this advice seriously, they should be able to come much more prepared and energized to each client meeting.

> –Eyal Benishti
> CEO at Ironscales

I like the constant reminders to keep the clients engaged and the discipline needed for us as sellers to make sure we keep executing flawlessly.

> –Kelly Miller
> Head of Partner Sales at Yelp

It's a really good, practical breakdown of sales process to help anybody in sales. As an experienced seller and manager of sellers,

it got me going back to basics to refresh and revitalise, and back to basics is always where you should go.
–Peter Gill
Director of Sales at Business Information Group

This book has a lot of good stuff that would be very helpful to early-stage sellers and great reminders for more experienced sellers.
–Joe Kuntz
CRO at Jobvite

I can tell just how much you care about helping others help themselves. I think your approach to sales coaching is very commendable and not at all overplayed. Most sales books are "how to squash to get ahead," but this is a very educational/ nurturing approach and I think you're going to be reaping the benefits for years to come.
–Crystal Grainger
VP of Sales at TrovaTrip

In reading this, I am humbled by how much I still have to learn in sales and how much I need to work on. This book was a great reminder of many sales tactics and I learned some new techniques to keep my skills sharp and customer engagement strong! A great read for new sellers and established sellers as well.
–Tom Watson
Channel Chief at TitanHQ

Great content and very applicable to all roles in sales. Great examples and the right amount of detail to understand the sales tactics and how to apply them in a practical sense.
–John Koopman
Global Direct, Revenue Operations at inriver

TABLE OF CONTENTS

What Others Are Saying — 3

About the Author — 7

Introduction — 8

How to Use This Book—To Improve Your Results Throughout Your Sales Career — 14

Top 10 Tactics—Every Seller Needs to Master — 21

TACTIC #1—Cultivating a Winner's Mindset: Becoming the MVP of sales — 22

TACTIC #2—Mental Preparation Before Each Call — 27

TACTIC #3—Prospecting and Mastering the Cold Call — 37

TACTIC #4— Right Now Contracts — 50

TACTIC #5—Presenting Value Props and Elevator Pitches with the G.O.L.D. Process — 60

TACTIC #6—Discovery Questions Using the F.A.C.T. Method — 74

TACTIC #7—Creating and Using a Business Case to Drive the Sale Forward — 88

TACTIC #8—Gaining Commitment on Budget, Timing, and the Decision-Making Process — 94

TACTIC #9—Overcoming Objections — 98

TACTIC #10—Give Yourself a Raise by Creating a Strong Referral Program — 119

Bonus Tactics—For Unique Seller Situations   127

    BONUS TACTIC #1—Partner/Channel Sales   128

    BONUS TACTIC #2—Sales Demos   138

    BONUS TACTIC #3—Selling to Enterprise Customers   147

    BONUS TACTIC #4—How to Rock a Tradeshow   155

    BONUS TACTIC #5—Always Be Coached   168

Conclusion   174

ABOUT THE AUTHOR

Scott Kaplan is the founder and chief coach at Quick Hit Sales T.I.P.S., a sales consulting company.

For over twenty-five years, Scott has helped countless sales professionals and executives across industries attack new markets, scale their go-to-market teams, and execute strategies for sustainable growth.

With a passion for helping sales teams excel, Scott has trained over 15,000 professionals on the foundations of sales management. His greatest professional joy comes from helping reps crush their quotas and double their bookings. He is widely recognized as an expert on sales tools to increase effectiveness, sales coaching, and go-to-market effectiveness.

INTRODUCTION

Everyone sells something.

You may or may not consider your primary title to be a salesperson; perhaps you primarily think of yourself as focusing on IT, marketing, or product design.

But trust me—you're still in sales.

That's what I've learned from training and developing more than 15,000 sales professionals throughout the course of my career. In a world of abundant, endless choice at the click of a button, when there are thousands of demands on our attention arriving on our pocket devices at all hours, there has never been a more urgent need to develop and master the time-proven skills that sales professionals rely on: the ability to tell a story, to explain how a solution meets a challenge or problem, and to close a transaction.

At the most basic level, all of us must sell ourselves in order to market our personal brands to employers, coworkers, and clients. Think about the requests you make for time from people in your network, or when you reach out for a LinkedIn connection, or when you put together a cover letter, or when you pitch an idea at work.

At the most fundamental level, you are selling the business of YOU—and making the case for why others want to be in that business.

The secret is how to use proven sales techniques and tactics for good, not for a quick buck or to rip off the customer. I believe at its very best, sales should be about problem solving. It is about finding the best possible solution for your customer! Too many people still think of sales as the stereotypical used car salesperson willing to say anything to make the deal happen. Sales is about being honest, ethical, and open with customers. It is about building relationships that are mutually beneficial and lead toward a common goal.

I've focused my life and career on training people to practice the art and science of sales the right way, so this is personal for me. I have found my passion helping sellers and sales leaders get better at what they do. For a quarter century, I have had the rare opportunity to partner with countless sales managers and sellers across a wide range of industries in every corner of the world—huddling with them on how to most effectively grow their sales skills, sales tactics, and refine their processes and teams in order to create winning sales environments.

But there's only so many people I can work with face to face, and only so many hours in the day. To really scale my impact and share the nuts and bolts of what I have learned with the widest audience possible, I knew what I had to do. I needed to put pen to paper about what I have learned to help those new to sales to hit the ground running and to help those experienced in sales to become the MVP of their sales team.

- Are you a rookie salesperson, unsure of how it will feel to be in the big meeting with a client? This is the book for you.

- Are you a seasoned pro, struggling to find new methods and approaches to breathe new life into your sales career to achieve quota, increase your commissions, and reach new levels of success? This is the book for you.

- Are you a manager or revenue leader, tasked with leading a sales team to greatness and help them meet ambitious stretch-goals that they aren't quite sure they are ready to hit? This is the book for you.

- If you see trends with giving discounts, pushing deals past your expected close date, or banking on that large "elephant" deal to hit your quota that you know will take a miracle to close—this is the book for you.

In short, anyone seeking to up their game and develop new mastery in their sales process will benefit from these actionable lessons; the value of learning is that you get the wisdom of others without having to make the same mistakes and errors that they faced along the journey.

We'll cover sales tactics: skills you can apply in certain situations to help your clients solve their problems, provide specific plans for sellers to focus on their development, and share ways to coach your teams to succeed well beyond what they could have imagined achieving.

Salespeople come in all stripes and forms from a wide range of backgrounds. Some study sales formally, while others find themselves thrust into the position with no experience. What is always true is that the professionals most poised to succeed bring a mentally strong mindset to push themselves and constantly learn to grow their abilities—and the same is true of those who will gain the most from this book.

To illustrate this, imagine I place a sixteen-ounce glass in front of you. Then I pour eight ounces of water in it.

You know the question I am about to ask you. How full is the glass?

The non-sarcastic answers tend to be half empty or half full. Before I give you my answer, let me ask a few more questions.

How full of water is the glass? What is the rest of the glass filled with?

Now you've got it.

Most people forget the second half of the glass is filled with air. So, the typical question to know if someone is a pessimist or an optimist is fundamentally flawed. The glass has always been full!

As the person who has always seen the glass as full, I am twice as optimistic, resourceful, positive, forward thinking, and creative than the "typical half-full person." As you read this book, challenge yourself to see the glass as completely full and be twice as productive, knowledgeable, and successful as the typical salesperson.

I pride myself on helping sales teams to double their bookings, but it's a two-way street to get there; the teams that succeed are those who are twice as optimistic and commit to being twice as productive, twice as resourceful, twice as knowledgeable.

I urge you to bring your "twice as. . ." mindset as you read and apply tactics from this book. Be honest with yourself and be critical in your self-assessment. Take a few minutes to answers these questions:

- What challenges are you facing in your career and approach to sales?

- Where do you excel, and where do you need to augment your approach?

- What got you into this business to begin with, and where do you find your passion on the tough days?

- What type of success do you want to have?

- Are you putting in the focused effort to learn, apply, and assess yourself to achieve those results every day?

I know firsthand how important these kinds of questions are. Very early in my sales career, I was coached by my mentors—many sellers and sales leaders, some who may not have even known I considered them mentors. It takes humility, curiosity, and patience to learn new skills, practice them rigorously, and master the multiple tactics professional sellers need to have.

My mentors taught me many lessons. They would tell me to get to the client's needs that matter the most to them to really understand what we were solving.

One of the first things I learned from my sales mentors were which questions to ask about the client's business to understand their current situation and any gaps they have.

They taught me what to listen for in the answers and how I should let the buyer answer the question instead of me giving the answer for them.

Over time, I continued to develop those questioning tactics in a way that let me understand the buyer's environment better than my competition did. I had insight into the impact I could have on the buyer's business, their priorities, and their ability to move forward.

Without even knowing it, I had developed one of my most important sales muscles and my own favorite sales skill. It even led me to develop the "F.A.C.T. Discovery Process" that we will discuss in detail later in this book.

As I started to train sellers, lead sales teams, and run sales operations earlier in my career, I quickly realized that I needed an effective selling process that was easy to remember so that sellers could effectively learn, adopt, and consistently use those skills and tactics throughout every client interaction and stage of their sales process.

I can promise you this—you will come away from this book knowing the fundamentals of the selling business. I have been steeped in the mysterious and always changing work of sales for years. I know the fundamentals like the back of my hand, and so will you.

But the rest of the equation will depend on you—on your readiness to take these lessons forward, on your level of commitment, and on your sense of urgency to begin implementing these lessons out in the field.

Let's get to it.

HOW TO USE THIS BOOK
—To Improve Your Results Throughout Your Sales Career

Before you can run, you've got to walk. And before you can walk, you've got to crawl.

For those new to sales (under five years), you will have limited experience, so you need to learn and practice the art of selling over and over. You will need to develop the necessary repetition to be successful in developing the multiple skills needed to be a great seller. Use this book as a daily or weekly guide to learn, practice, develop, enhance, and create your best practices. Learning sales is a process and takes time.

I look back on myself as a younger seller and thought I was the best seller after five to ten years of selling. I was wrong! I was great at certain parts of selling. I was great at making cold calls and getting clients to believe in me. I was great at a one-call close. I was great at selling a product that did not rely on supporting clients.

I was not great in enterprise selling as I needed more sales interactions, sales environments, client successes, and experiences selling different products to understand how to navigate a longer, more complex sales cycle. Luckily, as I moved into different positions and selling different solutions, I challenged myself to learn new skills and go through the process I mentioned above. I learned the skills through books, coaching sessions, watching others, etc. I learned what I was trying to do, why I needed to do it, the impact it had on customers, and what I would need to do to apply it in my sales role at that time.

I would practice on friends and peers. Then I would practice before client meetings. That led me to develop my approach with clients. I would do it over and over to see what worked and what did not. I would use those lessons learned (good and bad) to enhance my process, so I could consistently execute in different situations.

For those with a lot more experience, you have some strong skills that you have leveraged in your career thus far. But to be great in sales, you need to constantly learn and develop better ways to engage customers. I am hoping you are here to learn about new techniques and practices. You will get the most from the tactics within this book as you have the most experiences to pull from.

You remember the pain in years where you missed your quota, lost a deal you were sure you would win, pushed deals you were sure would close, or lost to the competition when you knew your solution was better.

As you go through this book, recall those situations and how you felt. If you get mad or angry—good! I want you to take an honest look at yourself and determine what you want to improve and then take action to make it happen.

I'm keenly aware that many who have only recently embarked on their sales journeys may pick up this book. So for them, it's important that we take a bit of time to review some of the more foundational elements of working and closing sales.

It's important for me to revisit the fundamentals myself from time to time. I started out in this business twenty-five years ago as my graying hair is all too happy to remind me. I recognize that the world has shifted and evolved considerably in the years since, especially regarding topics like technology and buyer behavior. It's important to stay humble and eager to continue learning new concepts along the way.

It's always amazing to me how a solid grounding in the core concepts underpinning sales can benefit you in virtually every aspect of your life, both at work and at home.

There's a lot of talk about what goes into sales. Young professionals and college graduates often ask me what capabilities they should be focusing on cultivating. The truth is that there's no silver bullet and no single tactic that will prepare you for every situation or room you will walk into throughout your sales career.

That's exactly what is so exciting about a career in sales to me— it requires a holistic, broad set of tactics drawing on technology, business savvy, and more—especially interpersonal tactics.

We often talk about the importance of "soft skills" like communication, empathy, and leadership. If you ask me, it's time to reboot the term with new terminology because that word *soft* implies that they are disposable or unimportant.

But nothing could be further from the truth—they are all critical in forging relationships, which is what any effective sales professional must do. You fall into a real trap if you are seen as operating in a purely transactional manner.

With so many qualified sales professionals out there who are perfectly capable of delivering on the bare minimum required, the real premium will always go to the salesperson who sees a human being on the other side of the equation. One who prides themselves on solving problems and forging a connection for the long haul.

You may be familiar with the "ABC" acronym popularized in business movies like *The Boiler Room* or *Glengarry Glenn Ross*— "always be closing." But for me, a much smarter way of thinking is: "Always Be Coached."

You only begin to decline when you start assuming that you know everything and don't need to continue investing in your development.

That includes coaching from a wide variety of people:

- managers
- peers
- your cross functional teams (marketing, product, buyer success, and executive team)
- and yes, in many instances, buyers

The best in the world at what they do—world-class athletes, business executives, world-renowned surgeons—continue to study their craft relentlessly. They never stop learning, they never rest on their laurels, they never stop looking over their shoulder. They attend seminars, read widely, study tapes of themselves performing, and make their development a personal priority in the midst of everything else on their schedule.

That's perhaps my single most important piece of advice. Be proactive in forming your personal learning plan—and so you should:

- Build a network of peers and mentors you can consult—and be willing to be there for others.
- Read books, articles, and social posts, both in your field and in other unrelated areas—you never know what creative ideas can emerge from the cross-pollination of topics.
- Go to conferences and seek out additional learning opportunities. There are so many options for learning and development, both in person and virtual.
- Seek out sales professionals with specialized expertise and experience—you can benefit from their mistakes without having to make them yourself.

I have had the honor of training more than 15,000 sellers and 5,000 sales leaders throughout my career. I have probably seen almost as many approaches to the job. But the one thing I haven't seen is a successful person who doesn't continue to push themselves to stay relevant. There's always more you can be learning and reflecting on. Even the best of us can get rusty or begin to rest on our laurels over the length of a career.

Hopefully, I have brainwashed you by now to know we all need to continually be growing and learning—lest we avoid being disrupted by the next trend or competitor that we didn't see coming.

On that note, let's start by learning what sales tactics we need to develop.

Let's start with a definition of sales tactic. Simply put, a sales tactic is a skill or set of skills that is used to develop relationships with buyers in a manner to sell them what they need or want.

So, with that definition, what sales tactics can you think of? Use the space below to jot them down.

_____

_____

_____

_____

_____

_____

_____

_____

_____

_____

_____

_____

Count them up. How did you do?

Did you choose tactics that are specific to sales or to the business world as a whole?

While a seller needs to know the tactic of listening, being a good communicator, and building trust, so do CFOs, HR managers, and engineers to be good at their jobs.

Understanding the specific tactics for sales, then developing your ability to execute with precision, takes time and focused effort. Regardless of your products or industry, professional sellers need to know what it takes to be successful. Here is a list I commonly share in my trainings to make sure sellers see the vast number of tactics they need to have to execute sales well. While I am sure I could list more, here are twenty that I work on with sellers all the time:

1. Territory Prep
2. Account Prep/Prioritizing
3. Call Prep—start a call, overcome objections, what to strive for
4. Elevator Pitches for company, team, product, etc.
5. Right Now Contract™ —setting agenda and expectations of each client interaction
6. Gaining interest so clients always want to listen
7. Qualifying the account, contact, and need
8. Overcoming objections
9. Learning and validating client needs via discovery questions
10. Getting commitments on budget, timing, and decision-making processes
11. Getting commitment on action items to move the sales process forward
12. Effectively positioning a "why change" message to get the client off status quo

13. Effectively positioning products/solutions—value proposition tied to the industry or role of your buyer
14. Effectively proving products/services offered to best solve the buyer's need
15. Establishing client references and referrals
16. Effectively working with internal/executive advocates
17. Effectively conveying product/service cost with value
18. Negotiating contracts effectively
19. Effectively communicating to the client what to expect going forward
20. Asking for the sale/closing

In this book, we're going to work on many of these tactics so that you can be the best damn salesperson you can be.

We will go through different examples and case studies. I will even provide a suggested seller action plan at the end of each chapter, so you can think about how to implement these tactics into your day-to-day routine.

Top 10 Tactics
—Every Seller Needs to Master

In my book (and hey, you are reading it), there are ten must-have tactics you need to master to maintain your relevance in today's changing landscape.

We see the world of work being rapidly disrupted and reoriented because of fast-moving trends like the global war for talent, the shift to distributed teams and working environments, and generational shifts, as we see five generations in the workplace en masse for perhaps the first time in the contemporary workplace.

Even in the age of emerging technologies like AI and machine learning, technical tactics alone aren't enough. And more than ever, what organizations need are people who are capable of integrating a wide number of technologies and practices into their work. Technology helps professionals optimize their work and big data can offer insights on making the right decisions. But you don't necessarily need to be a software engineer to have an appreciation for how technology can help you.

As technology increasingly automates routine parts of work, there will be a greater premium for the tactics that machines can't replicate, often involving strategy and leading people to buy—especially in Business-to-Business (B2B) scenarios.

So, let's dive into the tactics!

TACTIC #1
—Cultivating a Winner's Mindset: Becoming the MVP of Sales

When we're young, most of us dream as high as our imaginations will take us. We dream of being the best in the world at what we do—often in a lofty field like sports or entertainment. But as life whizzes by and we make inevitable compromises to balance our professional lives with everything else happening, we tend to lower our sights.

Where we once focused on excellence, now we are merely working on getting by, earning enough, and maintaining our position. This is one reason I see sales as such a powerful career path and opportunity to rekindle the fires of ambition.

Many professionals in other fields tend to correctly calculate over time that they aren't being rewarded in ways that are equal to their contributions. They can toil late and turn in flawless work, and the most they may be able to expect is a modest boost in salary that may not even keep pace with inflation.

But sellers work quite differently. They tend to rely on a model we can think of as "kill what you eat." That is to say, you can directly boost your personal bottom-line in the form of commissions and performance-based bonuses based on what you sell.

A great salesperson should be able to quickly find all the motivation they need to keep grinding, strategizing, and learning because they actually share in all of the rewards themselves in very tangible ways. Not that money is the only motivator, but it is a strong and common one in sales. It's therefore far easier to maintain a focus on being the very best when your game is sales—because you'll see the boost in your paychecks.

The first tactic you should focus on is cultivating the mindset of a winner. You have to believe in yourself and have the confidence to put a smile on your face and be relaxed with customers, so they want to engage with you. What does this mindset look like? What are some of the characteristics you'll exhibit?

- Determination and resolve. Sounds easy, but look at how you focus your time and energy into actions. You need to work hard and know how to work smart at the same time.

- The desire to be at your best. Whether that means knowing how you are better than the competition or you hate to lose (this is a big one for me). If I executed the way I needed to and lost, then okay. If I lost because I did not execute the way I needed to, then that loss is 100% my fault.

- A willingness to put in huge quantities of effort—what you need to do to get the job done. In many ways, sales is a numbers game as much as any sport. You need to be willing to put in the 10,000 hours that *Outliers* author Malcolm Gladwell argues is crucial to developing mastery at your craft.

- A patience and willingness to take the long view and invest time in your ongoing development instead of chasing every shiny object you see.

- Being open and honest with yourself. Throughout this book, I will challenge you to work on yourself and give you action plans that I suggest you use to develop your sales skills. Reflect and assess yourself after every client interaction to understand what you did and didn't do well. Get into the specifics of your performance and what you need to change going forward.

Of course, mindset isn't always the simplest matter to assess or measure. Someone can say all the right things, have good intentions, and work hard but fail to follow through when it counts. Or they may lack the grounding and wisdom to be able to put all the pieces together when it counts. Or they might work really hard but not in a smart, effective manner.

Remember—the glass is indeed full. It's always been completely full.

And that's the attitude a sales pro needs—not only twice as optimistic, but twice as productive, twice as knowledgeable, and twice as committed to getting the job done with their actions, not just their words.

The mindset of a seller is critical but all too often completely ignored. As sellers, your mindset is your drive, it is your focus, and it is your time to think about how to be the best seller you can.

Let's break it down into two pieces.

First, let's talk about our internal thoughts just before we start that buyer meeting. Your mindset results in the way you walk into that meeting. You must prepare yourself to walk in with the right attitude, demeanor, and drive.

As you read the list below, see what resonates with you. You can use a phrase like one of these as your motto to say to yourself before every sales meeting.

- Success or failure. . . it is a choice.
- Failure is not an option.
- Believe in what you sell.

- Think positively.
- It starts with your attitude.
- How am I going to stand out?
- Confidence is contagious.
- I help my buyers solve their problems, and I deliver results.
- I am the best seller out there. I care more about my clients, know more than my competition, and work smarter than any other seller out there.
- I am an excellent listener and problem solver.
- I sell with integrity, passion, and ethics.

Which of these phrases gives you the belief in yourself, your company, and your solutions?

Every seller needs to know the value they provide and have that in the front of their minds.

I even encourage you to say these aloud each day. Say it before each call or meeting. Say it even if you do not 100% know if it is true at this point. Keep giving yourself the positive mindset that you can make an impact to your buyer in that next call or meeting. You need to make it happen, and it starts with your mental BELIEF!

Sellers need to have the belief in themselves, their companies, and their products. Make sure you have that belief before each and every buyer interaction—no exceptions.

Suggested Rep Action Plan

Here is an easy tip to help. Set a calendar reminder for yourself that occurs every day for the first five minutes you are at work. In that reminder, add:

- The phrase(s) that resonated with you. Give yourself the BELIEF in yourself, your company, and your solutions. Make that your daily positive affirmation. Make it come to life in your daily activities. Even small steps forward each day make great strides forward.
- Keep yourself in a positive mind frame. Avoid negative conversations or people with poor attitudes as they will want to bring you down to their level.
- Surround yourself with like-minded professionals.

Suggested Manager Action Plan

Sales leaders—how are you ensuring that your sellers are prepared for each sales interaction?

One of the key responsibilities for frontline sales leaders is to coach and develop their team. As I mentioned earlier, the ABCs of selling should be *Always Be Coached* which means that the ABCs of sales leaders need to be *Always Be Coaching*. With that in mind, here are a few ways to help coach your sellers:

- In your 1:1s, discuss what gives them belief, confidence, and internal motivation.

- Catch them doing things right, so you help support the belief they have in themselves, the company, and your products.

- When you coach them with corrective action, give them examples on how others have done it correctly, so they can see what success looks like. Role play with them, match them with peers to practice, and give them recordings to foster their belief that they can and will improve.

TACTIC #2
—Mental Preparation Before Each Call

It's critical to go into any transaction, negotiation, sale, or meeting with the right preparation. You need to plan and visualize success. The same approach is necessary when getting ready for sales calls. Some of you might have heard of the "6Ps." Prior proper planning prevents poor performance.

I always ask any seller I'm working with to walk me through how they mentally prep for each sales meeting. They sound like basic questions, but you may be surprised how often they catch even sales pros off guard. I can't tell you how many countless times I've been on rides with sellers. Before talking with a buyer, I'll take a second and ask the seller, "What is it exactly that we're trying to achieve in this meeting?"

They'll often give me a look like "Scott, are you crazy?" They think it's an odd question because they're often thinking about the interaction solely from their own perspective. Of course, they know—or think they know—what the objective of the call is going to be. Isn't it as simple as making money and closing the deal?

What they are failing to consider is the client's point of view. What's this meeting about from their vantage point? If the meeting is nothing more than a way for the seller to line their pockets, that's not an especially appealing value proposition.

Over time I have developed a mental prep checklist—key points that I want sellers to really think about, so they can be as effective as possible on their next sales call. While some meetings require significant prep, many do not. Here are five items I recommend you make into a checklist before you call or see a client—let's name it our "five step call prep."

#1: What can I assume about this contact, company, and their needs?

Obviously, we need to validate the assumptions, but you talk to more of your buyer persona/profiles than your buyer does. Think about it. If your target person is the chief information security officer and you tend to talk to four people in these roles (or their direct reports) a day, then you are talking to twenty a week.

With some easy math, we can estimate that we are doing that for fifty weeks a year, which is 1,000 discussions a year. But consider the interaction from their side of the ledger; they will not talk to anywhere near that many information security professionals—and the few they do talk to are those who are dealing with the same issues and challenges, rarely with different perspectives and ability to identify the problem and solve it.

You, being the expert sales guru that you are, can leverage those multiple conversations so that you know the pains they have, the environment they live in, their limitations, the impact that software has on their business, their frustrations, and more.

Continue to consider what you know about your buyer's company. Know what they do, where they do it, and how well they do it. Know what industry they are in and what is going on in that industry today or in the near future. There is a world of information readily available. Do some quick research on their website, their LinkedIn page, and third-party data sources. Set up a Google alert and check their press releases. In general, do your homework.

To help you with making assumptions, consider the following when you do your research:

- Why do people buy your product or service?
- What type of account is this? Is this a new or current buyer? If this is a current or past buyer, are there any clues in their account history?
- What are your competitors doing or saying in the marketplace to create demand, disrupt the market, or attack your business?
- Are there any trends in the industry, vertical, or market segment?
- Is there anything going on in the local market?
- Are there any major events, tradeshows, publications, etc.?
- Are there any industry trends that come into play?
- What size of an account are you dealing with? (employees, revenues, locations, years in business, etc.)

Start every client engagement by putting yourself in your buyer's shoes and thinking about their needs, problems, and concerns.

#2: What value can I bring to help them?

Now that you have thought about **their** needs, think about what you can do to help solve those pains, needs, desires, frustrations, obstacles, etc. You bring value, so make a note(s) on how you can help them. This builds your confidence, and you must be confident before calling buyers, especially cold calling!

As you think about these solutions, be crystal clear in what you provide. Do not sell "speeds and feeds" of a product or service. Sell a solution to their problem.

Begin with a simple understanding of your client's needs. Think about what those features and the functionality of your products provide. Think about what services you are uniquely positioned to solve. You must know what pain you solve for people better than anyone else - so play to your strengths!

Does your offering solve or tackle their …

- Struggles to save money, control costs, and become more profitable?
- Desire to have more security, safety, reliability, or predictability?
- Fear, Uncertainty, and Doubt (FUD) about achieving desired growth plans or information security?
- Inability to connect with employees, partners, and buyers?
- Annoyances with manual tasks that should be automated?
- Feelings of being overwhelmed with multiple systems, processes, and procedures that do not work harmoniously?

If you do solve these types of concerns, then be 100% aware of how you do it. What results do you bring? How do you increase their capacity, capability, or results?

#3: How do you want to start the call?

Start with a bang! For the record, I am not talking about the pleasantries of starting a call. Saying hello, being personable, and being human is obviously a natural part of the sales process.

When you are ready to really start that meeting, you need to begin the call with a strong focus so your prospect/buyer immediately knows what you want to talk about. If you have an idea what their problems are and how you can help solve them, then start the call with talking about the pains you see in their world and lead them to how you improve their business, process, systems, people, team, Go-to-Market, etc.

Starting a cold call with no relationship is dramatically different than starting a call where you have been working together for years and have established rapport. That does not mean you should abandon your sales skills. In fact, the better the relationship, the better you can know their needs (less assuming, more validation) and the more you can help.

Starting the call sets the tone. You need to be confident and comfortable. That is where the planning comes into play. Plan out what you want to say, how you want to say it, and where you want to lead the conversation in that interaction. Here are a few tips to help:

a) **Tip # 1**—say it aloud three times. Repeat to yourself the thing you really need to say on this call. Maybe it is a "Right Now Contract™" (Tactic #4), a question, or a statement you want to validate. Saying it aloud gets you to say it in your style with the right tone and inflection. All are important!

b) **Tip #2**—be honest and blunt with your prospect/buyer. Bring up what you want to talk about. Get on the same page with your client and address their concerns and yours.

#4: What obstacles, roadblocks, or objections can you run into?

Be ready for hurdles and plan for them. Depending on where you are in the sales process, this will vary. The good news is that in each stage from prospecting to discovery, to prove/demo, to negotiation stage, there are probably only three or four objections you will hear 80 percent of the time. Plan for those and remember tip #1 above. Say it aloud at least three times.

Here are some of the obstacles that you might hear in your different sales "stages." We will review how to respond to these objections in our "overcoming objections" tactic chapter. For now, try thinking of the top objections you will get for each stage, so you can plan on how you want to handle those, either proactively or reactively, when you read that chapter.

- Prospecting stage
  - We have no need/not looking for anything right now.
  - I am not the decision maker.
  - We do not have time for this.
  - We are happy with our current solution.

- Discovery on introduction call stage
  - How are you different than your competitor?
  - Seems interesting, but this is not a need right now.
  - We do not have any money to spend. Budgets are frozen.

- Proof or demo stage
  - We do not have budget.
  - Your solution is missing something I need.
  - It won't work for us (tried this before, not ready for it, not sure what we need).
  - We need to do a trial/Proof of Concept (POC) first.
  - But your competition offers. . .

- Proposal Stage
  - It needs to go to procurement.
  - The price is too high / over our budget.
  - We are not sure we will get the value for the price.

- Negotiation stage
  - We can't get this approved (i.e. by legal, IT, Compliance, Security, CFO, etc.).
  - We need different terms (payment, length of contract, legal/contractual, etc.).
  - Can we get a few references to talk to?

#5: If everything went perfectly in this buyer interaction, what would I "sell" them?

I have found that over the years many sellers set lower expectations for each buyer interaction than they should. Set the bar high by asking yourself this very question, "If everything went perfectly in this buyer interaction, what would we finish with? What would be the next steps? What would I be able to sell them to move this deal forward?" Think big! Don't sell yourself short!

When I ask a Business Development Representative (BDR) this question, they typically give me an answer that involves setting a meeting with the prospect and their Account Executive (AE). And while that can be a part of the end game, it is not the picture perfect, ideal state that we would want if everything went perfectly.

So, let's amp it up! If we are thinking big, then we want to have a meeting set up with all potential decision influencers or decision makers because they are so excited to learn more that they are begging the BDR to set this meeting up as quickly as humanly possible. Now that is a way to answer the question if everything went perfectly in this buyer interaction.

If the BDR wants this, then they need to make it come to life. They need to have strong sales tactics that get people so excited that they want to see more. They need to have strong sales tactics that get people to want to invite their peers to learn more because of the value it provides to solve critical business problems. They should know which other people at that company should be invited by name, title, role, or business function.

When I ask AEs this question, they typically tell me they would close the deal. I understand that is the desire, but it is also a very easy answer with no thought.

First off, are you in a position that closing the deal in this interaction is even reasonably possible? For sellers that must go through multiple interactions with multiple decision makers and decision influencers, that is normally not the case.

Think about what sales stage you are in. What does perfect look like for that stage? How can you provide strong enough value to solve their needs in a way that pushes the deal forward?

Identify whether you need to engage other departments to better understand their pain, prove your value, scope the solution, create a business case with the decision maker (we will discuss developing a business case in a future chapter too), develop a ROI, or get executive alignment. Then make it happen. We will go through specifics in a later chapter on the "gaining commitment" tactic to break this down more.

My final note on this area goes back to the seller that says, "I would just close them." When I hear sellers tell me this in training, I challenge them to think bigger by asking, "If everything went perfectly, would you just close the deal?"

After some puzzled looks and hints from me, they realize that they would sell the buyer at full value, get a buyer endorsement, and get three referrals in the process.

So, before you start the next buyer meeting or phone call, ask yourself the following question. "If everything went perfectly on this call, what would I sell them and how would I make that come to life?"

Suggested Rep Action Plan

- Add to the calendar reminder you have each day with the 5-step call process. As you continue to go through your sales interactions, open that calendar "series" and add notes, examples, and buyer success stories you have so you can replicate great execution.

- You can open each individual "occurrence" in your calendar and make notes for the calls you have coming up. This will help you execute with precision in that buyer interaction. Be more prepared than your competition and outsell them every step of the way!

- Make it a priority to mentally prep for all meetings, even the most seemingly informal or low-stakes client conversations.

   o Share your prep with other members of your team who will be at the meeting and selling with you. This could be a sales engineer, technical Subject Matter Expert, or another team member, but all it takes is one unprepared teammate to throw a wrench in your plan and/or make your entire group appear unprepared.

- Make sure you begin every customer conversation with a clear understanding of their pain points and a concrete plan for your approach.

   o Consider how your competition will position themselves based on the client needs and what questions the client/prospect may ask.

- Anticipate any objections you might get in this meeting and prepare how you proactively or reactively overcome those (we will discuss overcoming objections in a future chapter).

- Strive for the best possible outcome by making it happen.

Suggested Manager Action Plan

- Set mental preparation as a key competency for your team. Ask members of your team to walk you through how they mentally prep for any sales meeting.

- Help them work through a specific piece of the five-step call seller process. For example, brainstorm different objections they might get and how to overcome them. Or help them to think big on what they can actually get in that buyer interaction.

- Highlight success when it works. Then they start to have comfort and belief in the five-step call prep process, so they have the desire to do it every day and before every buyer interaction. With that said, we all know that learning from mistakes is also a big part of our development, so when mistakes are made, go back to the five-step process to see what could have been done differently. That is a great lesson for future actions that will yield better results.

TACTIC #3
—Prospecting and Mastering the Cold Call

Prospecting for new business is one of the most difficult components of selling, and everyone's help is needed. That's why every buyer-facing team member should always be prospecting or assisting to making the prospecting efforts more effective.

Let's face it, cold calling is one of the hardest things to do in sales. You get a lot of rejection and have to convince people as you are interrupting their day. Few sellers like this part of the job. But it is necessary, and there are ways to make this more effective.

This chapter will break down every aspect with prospecting from setting up a prospecting cadence, to how to leverage that messaging to set up and execute an initial cold call with perfection.

In the most basic form, prospecting is about reaching out to new prospects or existing buyers to see if you can generate enough interest for them to learn more about your product or services. When done correctly, you'll get a buyer to take the desired action you're looking for.

Some sellers might want to set up the action to have an introductory call, and others might want to set up a product demonstration. Depending upon the request that you're making, it could also be to visit your office, to attend a lunch-and-learn, or to have them stop by your booth at the tradeshow you know they are attending.

It is about getting this passive prospect to want to engage with us. . . use our content, learn from us, see new opportunities, learn best practices, keep up with trends, and more.

When you are reaching out to prospects, you absolutely have to make your communications relevant, important, and valuable to them. Let's break down the prospecting actions we take and make sure we are familiar with each piece to get our desired engagement from that prospect.

As technology has increased, we have seen many software companies that exist to help drive buyer engagement. They develop "cadences" or "sequences" to engage clients, leverage best practices, measure response rates, A/B test different tactics, and provide intelligence on how to improve your success with your desired target audience.

So, let's start with a "cadence." While different systems can call it different things, the focus of a cadence is to know the type of message to send (phone, email, social), when to send it, and what to say. Many of these software companies that allow for cadences (e.g., Salesloft, Outreach.io., HubSpot, etc.) also have best practices, so look at their materials. Example cadences can be built for:

- Inbound demo request
- Inbound request for content download (e.g., e-book)
- Outbound for an event (webinar, annual buyer event, tradeshow)
- Outbound for cold calling for transactional sales (e.g., "one-call close")
- Outbound for cold calling for enterprise sales (e.g., account-based marketing toward your target ideal buyer profile)
- Outbound for a current buyer (e.g., quarterly business review, renewal conversation, etc.)

Regardless if this is a cold call to a new prospect or a reach out to a current customer, we need a seller to initiate the engagement with the client.

Example Cadence sequence for an inbound "demo request"

Note: these are business days.

	Day 1	Day 2	Day 3	Day 4	Day 5
Action	Within 5 minutes: Phone & Email: Schedule demo (they did request it)	Phone: Follow up #1 Offer assistance	Phone & Email: Follow up #2 Attempt to schedule	LinkedIn Connection w/ Message	Phone: Follow up #3 Still a priority with stronger Call-To-Action

	Day 6	Day 7	Day 8	Day 9	Day 10
Action		Phone & Email: Follow up #4 How we helped similar roles/companies	LinkedIn article, company post to share, etc.		Phone & Email: Follow up #1 Will take a break, will reach out in the future

Example Cadence sequence for an Outbound cold call/reach out to Ideal Customer Profile (ICP):

	Day 1	Day 3	Day 4	Day 5	Day 6
AM	Email: Ideal Customer Profile (ICP) Intro		Email: ICP Follow Up #1		LinkedIn Connection w/ Message
PM	Phone: Intro Call	Phone: Follow up call (no voicemail)		Phone: Follow up call (leave voicemail)	

	Day 8	Day 9	Day 11	Day 13	Day 14
AM	Email: ICP Follow Up #2		Phone: Follow up call (no voicemail)	Phone: Final Call (leave voicemail)	Email: Final Email
PM		Phone: Follow up call (leave voicemail)	Email: ICP Follow Up #3		

So, now let's think about the messaging. I will focus on the perfect email—as once you have that down pat, you can use that messaging for phone calls, phone voicemails, and social outreaches on platforms like LinkedIn.

Subject Line

While it might seem like a nuance, there are a few key items to remember in your subject line:

- Keep it short and sweet with no more than five words. Use a few words that describe the message and leave it at that.

- Mention your company—you can mention their company name too, but the message we are trying to send is how we best serve their company.

- Use strong verbs to help that message. Words like connect, partner, save with, drive, provide, etc.

Examples of this might include (assume your company name is "ACME"):

- Partnering with ACME
- Hoping to connect ** ACME **
- Connecting with ACME
- Driving e-commerce result with ACME
- Unmatched e-commerce data from ACME

The two strongest words to use in the subject line requires some pre-work.

- Use "Congrats"—this will double your response rate. But it must be genuine. Congratulate them on the company news, their promotion, starting the job, being highlighted in industry trades, etc. The more you know your buyers and keep good tabs on their business and industry, the better off you will be.

- Use "Referred"—this will increase your response rate six-fold. People trust their colleagues, so you being referred by one of them is a foolproof way to get a response. Ideally, the colleague will send the email introducing you to the prospect. But if not, you can say "referred by Scott" in your subject line. Again, be 100% honest here. We will cover this more in our "referral" tactic chapter later in this book. But know, this is money!

So, now we go to the body of the email.

- Greeting

    - Using "hey" or "hi" versus a more formal greeting of "dear" or "Ms./Mr." People like to talk to people who are less formal, so just as we use "congrats" because it is less formal, the same reasoning applies here.

- Email body structure—we need to break this down into three (3) distinct parts with one to two sentences in each. Do not include any marketing graphics as these can be caught by spam filters.

    - Relevancy—why should they even bother to listen to you? You must give them a reason to want to read more (or listen to you if you call). The more you tie to their industry, their persona, your expertise, the market dynamics they are encountering, etc., the higher likelihood they will continue reading.

- What we do—what you solve, what you help with, the results you provide. In a brief few sentences, you have to take all the guessing out of what you do. If the buyer is confused, even in the slightest bit, they will not continue and will delete your messaging.
- Call to action—product, persona/vertical, FUD (Fear, Uncertainty, Doubt). There is more information on that below.

- Phone messaging to follow email messaging for strength of message, ease to remember, and ability to recall name.

Call to Actions (CTAs)

A Call to Action is how you finish your message with a request to set up a clear next step. It is your ask. It is what you want to get from the prospect to move forward. Defining CTAs is easy, but getting people to take the action is the hard part.

The exact format and shape that these CTAs take can vary and so will the action you are requesting. When doing your reach out, start with asking, "What are you trying to achieve?" and "How can I best make that come to life?"

What is your CTA trying to achieve?

Some CTAs are informational (read a research paper, e-book, or case study or attend a buyer event, thought leadership, webinar, etc.)

Some CTAs are a direct ask (for time, connection request on LinkedIn, connection/referral to others, or an action for them to schedule time or answer a question).

Some people like their cadences to include up to three informational CTAs before a more direct ask. Both are acceptable and important, just understand the informational requests might slow down your engagement process.

Whichever you decide to use, make sure you track your responses, so you know what is working.

How do you make your CTAs effective to get the desired action you want? When you have a "Call to Action" in your prospecting, you must do much more than just ask for a time to meet. Think strategically about that request. How does the entire message (phone, email, social) lead me to making the CTA that the buyer will want to take (or at least agree to take)?

Who is it helping—you or the prospect? The request serves your purposes. Unless they are familiar with your product or service and are currently looking for your service, you will not create enough need or urgency for them to act.

Give them reasons that they CAN NOT SAY NO to your request.

Here are some T.I.P.S. to use to increase your response rate when prospecting to new prospects or existing buyers:

- Use active words in your subject line or start of your verbal conversation—strong verbs and using your company name in subject lines of emails or LinkedIn messages. Some examples are Connecting with, Partnering with, Donating to, Drive revenues with, etc.

- Ensure your message is relevant to the person you are reaching out to. Tie it to their role, their company, their industry, etc. Demonstrate you know their world.

- Clearly articulate what you/your products do. Do not make assumptions that they understand what you do, what you solve, or why they should trust you. You have to tell them. The hard part is that you must be concise, so pick a piece of what you do that you think will resonate best with that prospect.

- Be creative. I do not mean being silly or cracking jokes. I mean be creative in how you reach out to deliver that message. One effective strategy is the use of videos. Create a quick video that allows the prospect to hear your tone and passion to help and build the connection you are wanting to gain. It is easy to make videos with technology these days, and I recommend that your video image has a sign with your customer's name on it. Simple, creative, powerful, and effective!

There are also three calls to action that I recommend you use in your prospecting. You can use these as independent asks as well as merging them together. You can use these on cold calls, voicemails, emails, LinkedIn messages, or any other communication method. They are:

1. Learn about the product and service you provide specifically for their role, industry, and/or geographic territory/location.

   When doing this, make it as specific to them as possible. You want to leverage the expertise you have in solving their problems. Some examples could be:

   - "I have found that setting up thirty minutes to review how our product and service has uniquely helped solve (industry) challenges like (enter one or two key buyer issues for that industry). Please let me know when you are free in the next day or two for us to connect."

- "Our product has significantly helped (role) with (enter one or two key issues). They say a picture is worth a thousand words, but seeing a thirty-minute, high-level demo is worth a million words. Are you free tomorrow anytime from 2–4, or the day after anytime from 1–3 for a thirty-minute meeting?"

2. Share best practices, knowledge, concepts, and experiences you have with their industry and roles that show your industry expertise.

   Examples could be:

   - "We have worked with many companies in your (vertical) like (enter example company names). We listen to our buyers, and I would love to set up fifteen minutes with you to review some of the concerns they have and how they are solving them to help bridge any connections or resources that might be helpful for you. Do you have time now? Or can we set this up for tomorrow?"

   - "I often talk with (personas) and hear many stories and examples on how to solve their key business problems. Attached is a case study that I thought you might find relevant. I hope you find it helpful. You can let me know other resources you might need as well. If you would like to set up fifteen minutes to discuss this, please let me know what time works best for you. I am here to help you and (company name)."

3. Tie it to helping them make business decisions. This is where you can leverage people's Fear, Uncertainty, or Doubt (FUD) into their current thinking. FUD are all emotional pains that increase the likelihood for people to take action. Examples could be:

- "I talk with (roles) like you often and they always appreciate learning more, so they are armed to make better business decisions going forward."

- "Even if you decide not to go forward with me, this will help you make better business decisions going forward, especially in these difficult times."

- "Many (roles) have appreciated our initial talk as it helps them determine what to think about and plan for as they decide what business decisions to make or, more importantly, what decisions to avoid. Setting up thirty minutes to discuss these items will ensure you are considering the entire decision-making criteria for you to respond to market conditions and executive/board level questions, so you can weigh the options that might work for your business today or in the future. When are you free next week to have this talk?"

I encourage prospecting cadences to leverage each of these in your different messages. As you move into your fourth or fifth message in your cadence, you can start to use these in combination. Examples could be:

- "I would love to set up thirty minutes to review how our products help (roles) like yours. At this time, I can share what I am hearing from your peers, so you can leverage those learnings, best practices, connections, and resources to arm yourself to make more informed business decisions going forward. Do you have time now? Or can we set it up for later this week?"

- "What I have found worked for other (roles) is to review what we are hearing from our buyers like you. Then you can understand those perspectives and use that in your planning to respond to market conditions and business planning. This is critical in times of change and uncertainty. From there, maybe we can help with our solutions, connections, or partners. Do you have fifteen minutes tomorrow for a quick connect?"

Put all these items together in a cohesive message. Here is a cheat sheet that pulls these best practices together for you:

- Subject
    - Five words or fewer
    - Use your company name
    - Add strong verbs. . . partnering with. . ., connect with. . ., promote your services with. . .
    - When possible, use "referred by" or "congrats" to show connection, knowledge, and trust

- Greeting
    - Using "hey" or "hi" instead of more formal language

- Email body structure—three parts with one or two sentences in each. No graphics, one call to action:
    - Relevancy—to their industry, their persona, your expertise, etc.
    - What we do—what you solve, what you help with, the results you provide

> – Call to action—product, persona/vertical, FUD (Fear, Uncertainty, Doubt)

- Phone messaging to follow email messaging for strength of message, ease to remember, ability to recall name

Assuming you are following best practices, give your cadences at least three to six months or 500+ tries to gather data points before making changes/tweaks. When there is pressure to get more meetings, you will see sellers constantly changing their approaches and never knowing what works. So, leverage best practices and continue to learn from vendors who sell cadence and conversation intelligence solutions (i.e. Salesloft, Outreach.oi, Gong, Chorus, etc.).

Lastly, tone and emphasis are so important. You might have read something and added your own tone to it. One of the best sales operation and enablement leaders I have worked with, John Koopman, uses the example below to exemplify how tone and stressing items can create different meanings:

- IT'S not what you say, it's how you say it.
- It's NOT what you say, it's how you say it.
- It's not WHAT you say, it's how you say it.
- It's not what YOU say, it's how you say it.
- It's not what you SAY, it's how you say it.
- It's not what you say, IT'S how you say it.
- It's not what you say, it's HOW you say it.
- It's not what you say, it's how YOU say it.
- It's not what you say, it's how you SAY it.
- It's not what you say, it's how you say IT.

Be mindful of your sarcasm, humor, emojis, etc. They can create tone that might not be received well from your customer. Until you know the customer and how your style is perceived, err on the side of caution and be professional.

Suggested Rep Action Plan

- Develop your cadence.

- Write your email and use examples of each of the three key pieces to the email body structure mentioned above.

- Work in different CTAs.

- Practice using the similar message in calls, emails, and social connections so you have continuity of message.

Suggested Manager Action Plan

- Make sure your team has strong (a.k.a. validated with metrics) cadences for:

  - Cold reach out—cold call prospecting.
  - Inbound marketing follow-up—demo request, content download, etc.
  - Thought leadership—articles, industry news, analyst reports, etc.
  - Events—tradeshow, webinar, lunch-and-learn, etc.

- Measure the cadences to know the response rate, so you can develop a baseline and build cadences that achieve the desired results.

- Spot check to make sure they are following best practices.

- Leverage technology like SalesLoft, Outreach.io, Groove, etc. that help with the cadence automation, tracking, and synching with your Customer Relationship Management system (i.e., Salesforce, HubSpot).

TACTIC #4
—Right Now Contracts

What is a Right Now Contract? You may be asking yourself what exactly *is* a Right Now Contract?

It is not a new concept. It is something that I have seen in many sales methodologies. Sandler Selling system calls it "Up Front Contracts." Some have called it agenda and expectations. Many think of it as meeting management.

A Right Now Contract is how you establish the agenda, purpose, and desired outcome of <u>every</u> sales interaction with a prospect and/or customer for where you are RIGHT NOW in the sales process. Ideally, with mutual commitment from you and the buyer.

When done effectively, it provides clarity for the task at hand, builds alignment with those actively engaged in the buying process, and helps move the deal forward (or kills the deal, so you do not waste your time).

As you think about every meeting you will have with a client, consider the following question. "What do I need to do most effectively for where I am in the selling process and where the client is in the buying process?" It is what we need to do RIGHT NOW to get aligned with the buyer.

Right Now Contracts have three main components:

1. How we set up the meeting.
2. How we start the buyer meeting.

3. How we end the meeting with definitive next steps to move the call forward.

Like we discussed in our "5 step call prep," I do not mean that Right Now Contract should be the first words out of your mouth when you start a conversation. Meetings need to involve a degree of relationship building, lest you be seen as overtly transactional and simply focused on checking a box for a sale.

After you have the chitchat on the weather or weekend activities to build rapport, then when you want to start the meeting, begin with your Right Now Contract.

From this point forward, start every meeting with Purpose, Agenda, and Expectations.

- Purpose of the call
- Agenda of items to occur. This can also include the length of the call and any logistical items (e.g. location)
- Expectations—what is the desired outcome and expectation to walk away with from the discussion?

All Right Now Contracts need to be direct and honest with buyers. The better you get at leveraging this sales tip, the more honest you will become. By doing so, you will eliminate any ambiguity and ensure that there is absolute clarity on how to move forward.

You will be able to raise concerns and ask very specific questions on the deal process by establishing a consistent process of a Right Now Contract. Buyers will appreciate the open and direct manner, and they will respect your time more too. This is a great "win-win" where you can allow equal control of the sales and buying process.

This must be one of the top tactics that I have trained others on over the years—one that I know can be an instant game changer for your sales calls when used correctly. This capability is key to establishing an agenda, expectations, and outcome for every interaction that moves the deal forward without ambiguity. It is a tactic I recommend everyone use internally as well as externally with buyers when starting any meeting or conversation.

Put the Tip into Practice

To really see the value of Right Now Contracts, below are example scripts that you can easily adapt to your specific product or service.

Starting a call where you did not have a chance to set up the meeting:

There are sales situations where you are the first point of contact. These can be cold calls or follow-up to inquiries. These calls can also be when someone new joins the call/meeting that you have not met yet and there is no context set for the meeting. Here are some example scripts for these situations:

Cold call or a call with a new contact - "Hi Kelly, this is Scott Kaplan. I do not know if you are the right person or not. Is it okay if I get sixty seconds of your time and you tell me if I am in the right spot?" Then do your one-minute elevator pitch and ensure you end it with a transition question or action (see Sales Tip on Elevator Pitches). If your Elevator Pitch is thirty seconds, then say that. If it is longer than a minute, ask for a "moment." I have done this technique on thousands of sales calls or new buyer interactions, and 99% of the time I get the one-minute approval to move to my elevator pitch.

The key tactic here is to avoid the hang up where the buyer literally disconnects the call or mentally has checked out.

- The brief nature of this script allows for a quick answer for the buyer. And since I have not given any details yet, it does not sound like a sales call. I do not mention my company name or ask for anything more than one minute.
- It sounds like an inquiry—ensuring that they are much more focused on helping you.

Inbound Lead/Marketing follow-up: "Hi, Denise. This is Scott Kaplan from QHST. I see you requested some information. Before I go into too many details, is it okay if I take sixty seconds to review what QHST is so I know we are on the same page?"

Again, do your one-minute elevator pitch and ensure you end it with a transition question or action.

Please do not assume they remember what they read in an advertisement or saw on your website. Keep in mind: if this is a decision maker or decision influencer, they need to hear your elevator pitch multiple times to learn how to position your solution internally to get others involved, budget approved, resources assigned, executive focus, etc.

If you have already completed a meeting with the prospect or client, then you can easily set the stage for the next meeting. This can be set up by you or a different member of your marketing or sales team, like a business development representative.

Setting up a meeting - "So, when we meet next Tuesday at ten, we can review your goals, your current environment, and how QHST helps buyers just like you. At the end of that, we can determine if we think there is a fit and how we should move forward.

- Anything else you want to accomplish?
- Anyone else you want to join?

- Okay, I think an hour will work, so I will send a calendar invite over to you within a few minutes."

So, if you are setting up a meeting like that, then how do you think we need to start the meeting?

Here are a few scripts for how it can go down:

"So, when we spoke last, we agreed we would review your goals, your current environment, and how QHST helps with making your sales team more effective. At the end of this hour, we can determine if we think there is a fit and how we should move forward. Anything else you want to accomplish?

- As we go through this meeting, if you do not think there is a fit, are you going to be comfortable telling me that?

- Excellent. And, if there is a fit, you will be comfortable telling me that so I know we can move forward?

- Great—I will save five minutes at the end of our time to see where we stand."

As we start the meeting, we want to ensure we are going to have a lively dialogue. We are going to discuss what works and does not work.

You need to be comfortable asking for the "no" just as much as the "yes." This can take some time to get comfortable with.

There is also a degree of neuroscience to this process. By setting up the "no" versus "yes" situation with stating you will ask in the last five minutes for an answer, you are activating the "fight or flight" trigger in your buyer's brain.

The buyer will be more engaged, as they need to know by the end of the meeting if you are fit and why you are or are not the right person to help them solve their challenges.

This is a great place to have a buyer, as you will know if you have a deal or not and why. While asking for the "no" may initially feel a bit foreign, keep working at a way to make it more natural and comfortable for yourself.

Here is another script when starting a meeting for a product demonstration or service offering review. "As we go through this demonstration today, I am going to tell you about the top two to four items that have really proved to be of value for (persona/vertical) like you. Let's challenge each other on those items and ask each other questions to really see what works or doesn't for your business. I will save five minutes at the end of our hour today to review what points resonated with you, understand the impact it has on your business, and then determine if this is important enough for you to move forward with now or in the future."

As you can see in this example, I intentionally use "challenge," as it is a strong word. I then tie it to working or not working for your business. I use a specific word at the end of the meeting to leverage impact and importance to set the next steps (as you will see in a later chapter on the F.A.C.T. Discovery Process).

A Right Now Contract can also help you with keeping control during a meeting. Have you ever been in a meeting where things just feel like they are going down a different path than you had planned? When you feel that happening, leverage your Right Now Contract to get it back on track.

For example, you might say, "So, when we started, we agreed we would review your goals, your current environment, and how QHST helps increase sales effectiveness. It seems like we are going off on a different path, and I want to ensure we accomplish our goal. Do you want to table this for later to see if we have time at the end? Or can we extend our meeting for an additional fifteen minutes to discuss this now?"

If a buyer has fifteen extra minutes, then you have some more time to go off on the tangent. Or you can immediately set a new Right Now Contract as you found a more important outcome to your buyer. If they do not have the extra time, then bring them back to the task at hand.

The expectation you set for the meeting should always drive toward definitive next steps. The second part of the Right Now Contract is making sure you always have firm next steps, ideally with mutual commitment from you and the buyer. This is what we expect at the end of each call—a firm commitment of what the next steps are and a scheduled next meeting.

To be candid, most sellers do a horrible job finishing a meeting. They tend to lose track of time or do not want to sound pushy, so they do not lock down definitive next steps. Some sellers think they are doing well by simply getting another meeting on the calendar. But if you do not know the **Purpose, Agenda, and Outcome** of that meeting to come, then they are merely spinning their wheels.

That is why we always save five minutes at the end of each meeting to recap the needs and determine the next steps.

And since we set the expectations at the start of the meeting, we need to ensure we end a meeting effectively.

For example, "As we started the meeting, we said we would spend the last five minutes discussing if you thought we were a fit or not. To recap, we discussed how you (state any problems you found) and how we could help with (tie your solutions to their needs). So, let me ask you, are we a good fit?"

1. If no—"I am sorry to hear that, as I thought we were. Do you mind telling me where I missed the mark?"
2. If yes—"Great. I completely agree." From here you have two options:

   o "How do you envision us going forward?"
   o Just tell them what you recommend and get their commitment.

With this tactic, you get them to outline the next Right Now Contract and you say it back to them. Add any missing steps as needed. I love this approach. It appears to be giving the control up when in fact you will ensure you get the definitive next steps.

This tactic also gives you additional insight. If they are vague with next steps, then you need to make sure they know how to buy. Not every decision maker or influencer knows how to buy, so I like to use this as an indicator for what other details I will need to manage to get this deal closed.

I also like to do this as it can tell me if the buyer is being nice and saying "yes" when they really want to say "no," but they do not want to be rude.

So, you ensure they give you specifics. If they do not, then you give them specifics. Phrases like, "Normally what I have seen work best is that we set up an hour next week where I come to your office to review your specific needs and opportunities where you want to improve the business. Then we can outline a plan with a pricing structure that works for us both. After that, we can determine when the right time is to move forward, who would need to be involved, and how we need to get sign off from the business to move forward."

This is the definitive next step that I want, so I will just state it as the natural next step. This is also a great way to ensure that you achieve step five of our "5 Step Process." "If everything went perfectly in this meeting, what would I sell them?" Make sure your expectations and the outcome of the meetings drive to your perfect end game for that meeting.

A final note to those that sell in a more transactional manner, like a one-call close. While I refer to these interactions as meetings, it is very possible to have one meeting go through multiple steps of your sales process. As you transition from a cold call into an on-the-spot product demonstration into a request for payment and into a referral request, use Right Now Contracts as your transition statements. You can still go through all these sales step types in a one-call close.

Suggested Rep Action Plan

- Before each call, make sure you know what your Right Now Contract is and that you have expectations outlined for your meetings.

- Practice your Right Now Contract out loud before the call, so you can hear the purpose, agenda, and expectations.

- Ensure you keep to your Right Now Contract by getting agreement from the customer.

- Always leave a meeting with definitive next steps on how to move forward.

Suggested Manager Action Plan

- Ask your sellers for their Right Now Contract before they hop on a call.

- Ask your sellers how they used the Right Now Contract throughout the call.

- Ensure your sellers have a firm future commitment, so every call ends with a new Right Now Contract for a specific meeting with a purpose, agenda, and outcome.

- This is a great topic to use in a "huddle" with your team. Ask what the Right Now Contract would be for different sales scenarios. Use the above examples and add specifics like:

  o Cold calling a specific persona, vertical, referral, etc.
  o Starting a conversation for an introductory call, product demonstration, contract call, etc.
  o Completing any one of those calls and setting next steps.

TACTIC #5
—Presenting Value Throughout the Entire Sales Process

This is how to use value props, buyer success stories, and Elevator Pitches with the G.O.L.D. Process.

I have spent over twenty years working with marketing and sales teams at hundreds of companies developing the messaging for companies, products, and sellers themselves. It consistently amazes me how poor so many sales pros tend to be at this messaging.

There are many ways to think about how to present your value. But a tight elevator pitch can make all the difference. I would go as far as to say that using specific messaging that consistently provides value throughout the entire sales process is one of the most critical tactics a seller needs. And the beautiful thing is that there are so many ways to present value.

Let's break down the value propositions, buyer success stories, and elevator pitches to be more targeted and effective in providing value.

Most people think that you just give an elevator pitch at the start of a conversation, but I encourage you to give value throughout the entire customer engagement by having a process you can use throughout the entire cycle. In every conversation, you need to continually give and increase the value you provide to all decision makers and decision influencers. For clarity, let's define *value* as how I solve your critical business needs better than anyone else (including yourself).

Let's start with a structured process to the elevator pitch. I developed the G.O.L.D. process to give you an advantage in delivering your elevator pitch and value props:

The G.O.L.D. Elevator Pitch Process

<u>G</u>reeting of who you are (self and company) and what you do.

- What we do/offer as a company or as individual products
- Who you are (your role and experience)

<u>O</u>vercome Ambiguity with one or two points of value, importance, or validation to give you "street credibility."

- We need to give clients the reason for them to listen.
  - What issues we see clients have (in that industry or in that role)
  - How we solved it / how we help others like them
  - Benefit/what they can do now, so they take action

<u>L</u>ink to Need of their issues, concerns, and needs in the current market. We can provide relevant examples from similar clients, personas, verticals, use cases, geographic regions, etc.

- Have three main areas you help buyers solve (important business problems).
- Speak to each one using pain words like *challenged with, concerned by, overwhelmed with, frustrated by, struggling to, ineffective with, lack ability to*, etc.

<u>D</u>efinitive Next steps—we need to engage the client by moving the conversation forward. A smart seller will know where they want to take the call, so they complete the elevator pitch with an open-ended question or call to action to move ahead with the buyer (e.g., why should they change, engage, or hear more?)

Here are some examples my clients have used (I have redacted the company name):

Greeting: ACME Data Co. is a retail and e-commerce data software company based in Seattle, Washington. Our technology collects more data, collects it more frequently, and has more depth and breadth than anyone else in the market.

We can give you detailed data with two plus years of history on traffic to drive discoverability (organic traffic, paid traffic, keywords), conversion (content, ratings and reviews, promotions), and sales data at the brand, category, or product level across a retailer (Amazon US, Walmart, Target).

We give you near real-time data, so you can make educated decisions based on comprehensive data and facts, not educated guesses based on partial or somewhat accurate data.

Overcome Ambiguity

- We come from the biggest retailers, ad agencies, and consulting firms like Amazon, Walmart, and Boston Consulting Group.
- We have over 5,000 buyers around the world—some of the largest brands as well as smaller ones that achieve 50% greater results than those that do not use our data (we know because we track it).
- We are the only data provider that uses true data science with multi-variant modeling to look at numerous sources to estimate purchase intent that we constantly validate.

Link To Need

To give you some specifics, when we work with brands like yours, we typically help them solve a few **common problems**. For example:

- Brands are **not aware** of their performance compared to competition and are **annoyed** they cannot create a more effective strategy based on detailed competitive and market data to predict and achieve sales growth.
- Brands **struggle** to measure category performance by sales volume, traffic, conversion rate, price, promotions, and market share across their e-commerce retailers to know what will really drive purchase intent.
- Brands are **overwhelmed** with how to scale and grow across a retailer to increase market share or profitable growth across a category or sub-category.

Definitive Next Steps

So I can tailor the rest of this conversation to you. . .

- Which one of these are you experiencing the most?
- This is only scratching the surface. What are the key priorities you are currently focusing on to increase your e-commerce results?

Here is another example from a completely different industry

Greeting

The true value of ACME Financial is transforming the way capital markets' operations are conducted by providing the network and ability to optimize collaboration and data-sharing. Our content agnostic platform allows data to be ingested in any format. This data is then normalized and published to provide data collaboration, workflow automation, and technology efficiency across your ecosystem.

Overcome Ambiguity

We are the **only** company that has a network of 4000+ unique firms that does over $1B in monthly transactions.

We are fortunate to have many clients like JPMC, Citibank, Barclays, Goldman Sachs, and Credit Suisse.

Link To Need
Often when I speak to (personas/company type), I hear that they are:

> **Struggling** with all the disparate systems, so they live in a world without real-time data collaboration, at scale, that allows them to minimize risk, reduce costs, gain benchmarking insights, and enable expansion.

> **Frustrated** as their band aid processes are fragmented, they are unable to quickly collaborate and simplify transactions. Their infrastructure does not allow their participants to work in a single environment for decision-making and resolution of transactions.

> **Concerned** about how to address the challenges while remaining competitive, especially as new financial services technologies continue to emerge.

Definitive Next Steps
Which of these struggles is most important to talk about first? How do you see these areas limiting your ability to achieve the business results you want?

Your Turn
Write two or three bullets for each piece of the G.O.L.D Elevator Pitch Process. Do not write full sentences, as I have found too much scripting is just that. . . too much.

Get the main points down here—don't overthink it.

- **Greeting**—*Who you are (self, company, and products) and what you do*

- **Overcome Ambiguity**—*One or two points of value, importance, validation*

- **Link to Need**—*Issues, concerns, needs in the marketplace*

- **Next steps**—*Open-ended question or call to action to move forward.*

Now that you have your elevator pitch, let's discuss how to best use it.

- You want to be concise and engaging. Try to tell it in a story about the value you, your company, or your product(s) offer and the business problems you solve.

- When you get good at using this structure, it is easy to take pieces and use them throughout conversations. For example, you might bring up a challenge and finish with a question to drive engagement. Then include a feature, function, or solution you provide better than anyone else in the market.

- When to give elevator pitches/value propositions:
  - First contact with a buyer to see if they have a need
  - To mention additional offerings
  - Start of a conversation/meeting
    - Introduction of product
    - Start of a demo
    - New contact that has joined the meeting, and you want to give them the high-level overview of your product or company
    - Start of meeting to bring value to the discussion
  - At the end of a meeting—tied to their pain/needs
  - Throughout a presentation or product demonstration—tied to their pain/needs
  - When delivering prices/proposals—tied to their pain/needs to show how you solve that need better than anyone else in the market

- How to deliver elevator pitches:
  - Enunciation and speaking clearly is a must.
  - Pace and tonality—you hear your elevator pitch all the time, but people hearing it for the first time need time to process what you are saying.
  - Have inflection—verbally and with body language. You want to stress a key message, so it resonates. For example, if in your elevator pitch you are highlighting three points, use your fingers to highlight one, two and three.
  - Keep your diaphragm open—do not cross your arms and keep your head up and maintain eye contact.
  - Have personality—smiles, eye contact, energy, and passion are critical. It makes you sound unique and likeable. Even in today's age of

technology and mass communications, people still want to buy from people they like.

o The power of a story—make it personable, know specifics, and have examples that make it relatable to your buyer. It helps build confidence and connection to your buyer.

Here are some tips on how to effectively use value props and elevator pitches. This time, I will use examples from my own consulting business.

- Cold call example:

  o "Hi, Cameron. I am not sure if you are the correct person I should be speaking with, so can I take sixty seconds to explain why I am calling? Then you can tell me if I am in the right place? Thank you. My name is Scott Kaplan, and I am the founder and chief coach of Quick Hit Sales T.I.P.S. We are a sales consulting company that helps businesses with the go-to-market sales strategy, and we provide targeted sales training and coaching for sellers and sales managers.

  o "We have been developing sales processes and best practices for over twenty years and have trained well over 15,000 sellers and 5,000 sales managers. We help sales teams achieve double to triple their current results with tools and best practices they can use on their next buyer conversation!

  o "Typically, when I talk to chief revenue officers like you, I hear they are struggling to get their new sellers to ramp up quickly. They are frustrated with deals consistently slipping and missing their forecast and are tired of hearing the same sales mistakes from their sellers and managers. I am curious to know how you are experiencing these situations and what you are doing to resolve them?"

- Inbound call from a marketing lead—first call:

  o "Thank you, Rachel, for requesting (some information/our demo/downloading our data sheet). Before I get to your request, I am going to back up for sixty seconds and explain what we do at Quick Hit Sales T.I.P.S., so I am sure we are on the same page.

  o "Quick Hit Sales T.I.P.S. is a sales consulting company that helps businesses with the go-to-market sales strategy and provides targeted sales training and coaching for sellers and sales managers. We have been developing sales processes and best practices for over twenty years and have trained well over 15,000 sellers and 5,000 sales managers.

  o "We help sales teams achieve results with tools and best practices they can use on their next buyer conversation!

  o "Typically, when I talk to chief revenue officers like you, I hear they are struggling to get their new sellers to ramp up quickly, frustrated with deals consistently slipping and missing their forecast, and they're tired of hearing the same sales mistakes from their sellers and managers."

  o "I would love to hear some of your concerns, so we can tie this conversation to your needs. What are some of the issues holding you back from achieving the results you want or need to achieve?"

- New Contact example:

  o "Nice to meet you, Connor. I am glad that Dede asked you to join this call. Before I go further, let me explain what Quick Hit Sales T.I.P.S. is, so I know we are all on the same page.

  o "My name is Scott Kaplan, and I am the founder and chief coach of Quick Hit Sales T.I.P.S. We are a sales consulting company that helps businesses with the go-to-market sales strategy, and we provide targeted sales training and coaching for sellers and sales managers. We have been developing sales processes and best practices for over twenty years and have trained well over 15,000 sellers and 5,000 sales managers.

  o "We help sales teams achieve results with tools and best practices they can use on their next buyer conversation! Typically, when I talk to chief revenue officers like you, I hear they are struggling to get to get their new sellers to ramp up quickly, frustrated with deals consistently slipping and missing their forecast, and tired of hearing the same sales mistakes from their sellers and managers. So that I can tailor today's conversation specifically to you, can you please tell me your role and what resonated with you?"

- Later in the sales process, you will find yourself in a meeting where you are proving your value. Some people do this in their discovery calls, while others do this in their product demonstration. This is a great time to use this

G.O.L.D. Elevator Pitch Process to help you get deeper in your conversations with buyers. Here are some examples:

- o "Jessica, one thing we have not discussed yet that many of my clients care about is some of the struggles they have with. . . (insert pain point). How are you handling this? Is there any significant problem in your business that you would love to solve?"

- o "Sara, I was talking to one of my other buyers and she brought up a great point that I would like to share with you. She was really concerned with. . . (insert pain point). The more we talked about this, the more we realized how important the solution we could help provide was for her. I would hate to not discuss the items that are really a priority for you, so please let me know if I miss anything. Let's add onto our discussion, so I can understand your full scope of needs and priorities. Do you have a similar pain point and priority like she did? Or have we already addressed your main priorities?"

These examples just scratched the surface of how we start to deliver value. But the more you know about your buyer's market, the verticals that they play in, and the personas that you're working with, the better you'll be able to provide value added positioning that finishes with a question to better engage your buyers.

As you read through these examples, did you notice:

- • The basic consistency of the message? That makes it easier to use the messaging and remember the key points.

- The consistency of the message is also easy for the customer to remember and then use when they have to sell internally to get resources, attention of peers, funding, or approval.

Common Myth of an Elevator Pitch

There is a common myth that an elevator pitch needs to be less than thirty seconds or sometimes even fifteen seconds. That is a myth more often than a fact.

The only time you are "on the clock" with your elevator pitch is when you're on a cold call and ask for sixty seconds of their time.

However, think about how you engage clients in meetings and discussions that is not a cold call. More often than not, you are going to talk with them about a specific feature of your solution or company for two, three, or five minutes, if not longer.

I find that sellers often put undue pressure on themselves to rush through an elevator pitch instead of doing it effectively.

Customer Success Stories

Many sellers like to think about the positive impact they have on customers. They like to share those stories. Telling examples of similar buyer roles and similar industries that decided to use our product gives the seller confidence and builds trust with new customers.

So, another great tool for presenting value are customer success stories. Like our G.O.L.D Elevator Pitch Process, we have a similar structure here to remember how to effectively convey value through our client stories.

First, start with the issue the client had and feel free to use the pain words we discussed earlier.

Then talk about how the client solved it using your product or services in a way that nobody else could help them.

And finally, finish with what they're able to do now. Bring up the key metrics or issues they wanted to solve so that you can highlight the benefit of using your product or services within that environment.

One thing that is uniquely different about this structure is that you're talking about a client and telling a story, so bring in the details and the specifics to enable you to really convey what the client went through.

That doesn't mean it has to be a long story or even about a client that you specifically sold. And just like we did with the elevator pitch, we finish with a question to engage our buyers.

Here's a basic framework for you to follow. See if you can fill in the gaps and jot down at least one solid client case study.

CLIENT CASE STUDY STRUCTURE

* A client had issues with: _____

* How we solved it: _____

* What they can do now: _____

Weave this structure into a story to get the client to listen...and finish with a question.

Suggested Rep Action Plan

- Develop your elevator pitch—write it out to help you. Write one for your company, yourself, and your main products.

- Say it out loud ten times a day for the first week and then three times out loud at the start of each working day (put it in your calendar).

- As you get more comfortable and fluid with it, adjust your pitch based off of different personas, verticals, products, buyer use cases, etc.

Suggested Manager Action Plan

- Ask your sellers for their personal, company, and product elevator pitches.

- See how and when your sellers present value. Pay close attention to how they are constantly presenting value that meets the client needs in meetings, as well as post meeting follow-up communications.

- Talk about the different value props used throughout the sale cycle at team meetings and huddles to collect feedback.

- Remember to celebrate wins! Assess what drove your success in each situation. Replicate that win and share with your peers/sellers to see how to apply it to a new task/situation.

- Share successes and lessons learned with your team (e.g., take five minutes in each team meeting to review a tactic and how you applied it successfully).

Tactic #6
—Discovery Questions Using the F.A.C.T. Method

Asking questions is a critical part of the sales process. Flying by the seat of your pants won't work in a sustainable way when you are playing in the big leagues. You need to know what the right questions are to ask, when to ask those questions, and what you're trying to get from the answers, so you know what to listen for.

These questions play an important role in helping you discover your client's pain points and how you can provide value.

Discovery questions occur throughout the entirety of the sales process. Being prepared to know what you want to ask and what you're trying to uncover are critical steps in the pre-call planning and during the sales meeting execution.

In this chapter, we're going to break down the types of questions to ask. We'll also take a look at plenty of examples of how to ask the questions, so you can be effective in your next sales meeting.

I use two different types of questions. They are qualification and discovery questions. Let's define them:

- Qualification questions are the questions you ask at the very beginning of the sales process to determine if this is an opportunity worth pursuing.

- Discovery questions are the more in-depth questions where we will spend most of our time.

For qualification questions, I train sellers to make sure they know what information they need to gather in the first five to ten minutes of an engagement process to determine if this is even a deal that they should be working on (or for a sales development rep/business development rep to provide as a valid lead).

I like to break it down into three sections and will provide some examples of things to consider (adjust based on your environment):

1. The company—What is the company? Where are they located? How many locations do they have? How many employees are there? What geographic locations do they serve?

2. The contact—Their name, title, role in the buying process, role in the decision-making process, and their team.

3. Their need—Why do they want to learn or see more? What are they doing now? What are their short-term needs?

The following is an example I built when I worked with one of my clients selling medical industry solutions:

Company	Contact	Need
What is the company? (Hospital or Health System)	Who is the person?	What are you doing now for your telehealth process? Who are you using? Working/not working?
Where are they located? How many locations?	What is their title/role?	Who else is experiencing challenges with your telehealth process? What specialties?
How many specialties?	Are you responsible for deciding which technology vendors you need?	What is the main business driver behind this project? Budget given yet?
Volume/patient load? # providers to support?	What is their role as it relates to technology investments?	Why do you want to learn more/see a demo? Desired outcome?
What is your net patient revenue?	Who else is involved? Titles? Involvement?	Do you have any specific needs you are trying to solve in the short term? (Ask what short term means to them.)

Now onto discovery questions.

In simplest terms, discovery questions are solution-based questions that help us frame the need, drive buyer commitment to action, and uncover the client's urgency to take those actions.

These are the deeper level questions that we ask in "introduction" or "discovery" calls, during demo, and post demo. . . ideally through the entire buyer lifecycle. They are a critical tool in better understanding where your buyers are coming from and forming long-term relationships. The questions need to be conversational and fluid. No one likes to be bombarded with question after question.

Very early in my sales career, I was coached by many sellers and sales leaders to ask questions. They would tell me to get to the client's needs that matter the most to them to really understand what we were solving. I imagine it's a good tactic to know for many different kinds of professionals, from doctors to journalists.

My mentors gave me some truly great tips on questions to ask about the client's business to understand their current state and the gaps they have. They would give me great advice on how I should let the buyer answer the question versus me giving the answer for them. I read books like *Spin Selling* to understand different types of questions and their intent.

I continued to develop those questioning tactics in a way that enabled me to understand the buyers' environment better than my competition, the impact that I have on the buyers' business, their personal priority, and their ability to move forward.

This became my favorite sales tactic to develop, practice, and use! It helped open more doors, build more alignment, and increase my sales velocity (time to close a deal) and the average value of my deals.

As I started to train sellers, I quickly realized that I needed a process that was easy to remember, so they could effectively use those questions throughout the entirety of their sales process in a fluid, comfortable manner.

I have continued to refine it and have provided thousands of sellers with detailed questions and a questioning process—allowing them to ask better questions, elicit better answers, and be more effective in their sales meetings.

So, let's break down this question process.

I'm a big believer in acronyms. They are a means of remembering an effective process or tactic to use. To that end, I call this process the F.A.C.T. Discovery Process because we want to get the facts needed to move forward.

The F.A.C.T. Discovery Process can be boiled down to:

> **F-** Fundamentals of the business
> **A-**Ability to move forward
> **C-** Commitment level
> **T-** Timeline to act on commitment

F = Fundamentals of the business

These are the questions that are technical, data driven, or explain their history/current state. These questions play a critical role. They help to FRAME THE NEED/PROBLEM.

Think of the history or data points we are trying to uncover or possibly the technical issues that the buyer is experiencing. Think of the questions below (you can provide more text for your own knowledge by adding in specifics for your business):

- What do you do when. . .?

- What is your process for. . .?
- How do you. . . (measure/track/respond/handle/perform function "X") today?
- Where do you. . . today?
- How many. . .?
- Do you have. . .?
- How often do you. . .?
- When "X" happens, what is your response?
- How do you use (system, tool, or process) today? How is it working for you? Any issues?

These questions gather the necessary historical context and business insight to better understand the opportunity at hand. FUNDAMENTALS gives you data or business insight to FRAME the need / problem.

Sample "F" questions that I have used with one of my financial services clients are below. You can use these as needed.

Some examples of "F" questions include:

- How do you plan for *exemptions* today?
- What is your process today for *finding exemptions*— Who is involved? What is their process? How effective is it (steps, quantity of emails, time, gaps, etc.)?
- How do you get access to *real-time transaction data— gathering, aggregating, and tracking status?*
- How do you prioritize *workflows?*
- What are you doing in terms of *reports, communications, etc. with your clients?*
- How do you look at your *risk in your transaction? And how do you control your risk?*
- How are you preparing for *government regulations?*
- *How do you handle* (enter their stated pain point) *today?*

The good news is that most sellers are really good at these fundamental questions.

They have a long list of questions to ask and continually ask them to their clients to get a great framing of the need.

The bad news is that sellers are typically not good at asking the rest of these types of questions we are about to go over. So, as you read on, be honest with yourself in terms of the types of questions that you ask and what additional questions you want to start to ask.

A = Ability to move forward

These are the questions that tell us how a buyer is going to move forward in the buying process. We want to ask detailed questions and not make any assumptions with regards to their decision process, decision makers, time frame to decide and then implement, the competition we are going against, and their ability to buy our solution in their company.

Sellers are typically poor with getting the details here. They might ask a question or two but rarely are comfortable enough to ask the more detailed questions and ensure they get the answers. As a confident seller, you need to make sure the alignment to move forward is clear on every aspect. Learn to ask these questions in a calm, confident, and fluid manner.

Before we go through the different types of questions to ask, I want to make sure that we're being clear on when to ask these "A" questions. We typically need to do a few things first—framing the need, understanding the business impact, and knowing the person's personal prioritization.

So, do not think of F.A.C.T. as a chronological process for asking questions. The "A" questions are best used after the "F, C, & T." Obviously, you might ask some of these questions up front, but the detailed questions will come a bit later in the sales engagement.

Example of "A" questions include:

Buying and Decision-Making Process
- How does your company evaluate new products or services before buying?
- Will anyone else be involved in this decision?
- Are there any upcoming events/deadlines that you'd like to have a solution in place by?
- Walk me through your decision-making process.
- What is your role in the decision-making process?

Time Frame
- What is your timeline for getting started?
- When do you want something in place?
- Walk me through your timeline for evaluations, decision-making, procurement, installation, adoption, and training.

Budget Process
Let me first make note of something—far too many sellers are afraid to ask questions about the budget.

You will need to overcome that tendency and be able to dive into specifics.

In order to understand your buyers' budgetary needs, focus on questions like:

- Have you identified a budget range for this investment? How heavily will price factor into the decision?
- What's the process for obtaining the budget and who would be involved?
- What do you currently spend now on this problem or need? Whose budget is this coming out of?

And finally, the last piece of Ability to move forward questions.

Competition

- What other solutions are you looking at?
- Where are you in your evaluation process? What is your process?
- What other vendor solutions do you currently have in place?

These are just a few samples of the questions you need to ask. Are there others you can think of? Any other questions you have found to be effective? If so, add them as noted in this book, so you can use it as a reference to prepare for meetings, execute on meetings, and evaluate post meeting how well you did.

C = Commitment Level

These commitment-level questions assess the business impact. These are the questions that help us determine the impact our solution has on their problem. These questions will help us understand what actions our buyer is willing to commit to.

We need the business impact to be substantial enough that the buyer is committing to action to buy. Think about the action you need to see from a customer to buy and how committed those customers are to taking each one of those actions.

We'll see that come through with commitment actions like seeing a demo, giving you access to cross functional decision makers, setting up time to drive toward implementation, preparing resources to get a contract through legal, getting IT to sign off on the proposed software solution, etc. All of these actions show commitment to solving the problem and getting the solution in place.

These tend to be the most difficult questions for sellers to ask AS WELL AS get answers for. It tells us what they have to gain or what they have to lose, so we know what actions they will commit to. The best way to drive buyer commitment to action is to quantify the personal, departmental, and business impacts.

Consider using words like *impact, hinder, limit, affect, gain, achieve, benefit, receive* in your questions.

Example "C" questions can be found below. You can fill in the details for your business:

- What impact is your current process/software having on your. . . people, process, systems, department, financials?
- What would be the impact to the business/people/teams to be able to. . .?
- What's hindering you from getting to where you want to be today?
- What would you be able to achieve if you were able to. . .?
- How would (feature/function) be beneficial to your business/people/teams' ability to. . .?
- How would this be beneficial to the level of service you provide?
- How would the combination of. . . allow you to provide more capabilities for your clients/teams/business?
- What do you want to achieve going forward that you cannot do today?

Here are some questions I have seen clients use that are specific to their business:

- What impact is automation having on your systems and processes from a change management perspective?
- How are your current systems and processes hindering your ability to understand data, prioritize work, and solve transaction issues now?

- What type of communication and access to real-time data would you like to have? How would that improve things going forward?
- How would automation with creating rules and managing your risks benefit your business/workload/client satisfaction?

Since we have talked about the importance of "selling to pain" in previous chapters, the words *impact, affect, hinder,* and *limit* are the pain style words to use to help us get to what they CAN NOT DO today.

These questions and answers help us quantify that pain and develop ROI by talking about the results they want to get versus the results they are getting today.

As you continue to get better at these questions, you will see how to use them as a lead in for a topic. For example, "Mr. Buyer, before I start to show you our product/service, I want to make sure I am making it specific to your needs. When you look at your current situation (tie it back to your product/service), what is limiting your ability to achieve the results you want?"

This is an excellent way to ensure that you go forward in that conversation in a way that ties directly to the buyer's needs and where they want to make changes. This drives their commitment to take the action of change.

I know some of my sellers out there like to play to the positive side. So, after you show a strong product feature or functionality, finish with a positive-based, commitment-level question. That is when we can use the words like *gain, achieve, benefit,* or *receive.*

For example, "If you had the ability to do (enter product/service specific features or functions), how do you think that would help you? What would you gain that you could not do today?"

T = Timeline to Act on Commitment

The final set of questions helps us determine where it falls on their priority list and what the level of urgency is to act now. Urgency, of course, is centered on the buyers' timeline to act on the committed change.

And as sellers, we want to drive the buyer to act with urgency.

The best way to get commitment from the buyer is if they convince you and they convince themselves that finding a solution is a very high personal priority as well as a business priority.

By going through the proper questioning process, a good seller can take an issue and magnify its importance so all buyers (business, economic, IT, legal, executives, etc.) move forward in the buying process.

Example "T" questions include:

- What are your top priorities at the moment? Where does this fit on that list?
- Why is this a priority for you now? -or- Why would you commit time and resources to something that's low to medium priority?
- How important is this to you? What about other departments/executives?
- What gaps are you trying to fill/fix today/this quarter?
- How important is (process/result/feature/function) to you to fix/change/improve?
- On a scale of one to ten, where ten is something you need to do now, what would you rank the need to implement (feature/function/solution)?
- How do you measure your/your team's success?
- How important is. . . for you to solve within the next ninety days?

- What initiatives are you currently working on? Are those tied to major company initiatives?

Don't forget that the questions need to be conversational and fluid. No one likes to be bombarded with question after question. Some examples of how to make these conversational are:

- So that I can make sure I only give information that is relevant for you, let me ask you. . .
- I would like to make sure I am tying our conversation to what you are working on so. . .
- What I have heard from other (personas or vertical) is. . . how does that relate to your business?
- If I go a little deeper into what I heard you say. . .
- Can you please elaborate on that? Any idea the impact it is having on. . .?
- That is a lot. . . how do you prioritize?

The person who asks the best questions wins. So, double the number of questions you are asking! Ask questions with more intent. Be more cognizant of the answers you're getting to make sure you get the level of detail you want in the commitment level from the buyer to move forward.

And remember, just like our other techniques, you need to prep and practice. So, make sure you have your questions outlined and practiced before your call.

Suggested Rep Action Plan

- Practice to ensure you ask all four types of F.A.C.T. questions. You want to practice the question as well as listen for the answer that you wanted.

- Practice with your accountability partner—someone who will keep you honest and make sure you are fully leveraging your process rather than taking shortcuts because "nobody is looking."

- Prep AT LEAST three questions you want to ask before each meeting (thinking about where you are in the sales process and where the buyer is in their buying process) and practice them out loud three times right before the meeting.

Suggested Manager Action Plan

- Ask your sellers for their questions and see what they have uncovered on their buyer calls. Practice these questions with your sellers before the call, so they are confident.

- See how your sellers are leveraging the information from these questions to present unique value to their buyer. Ask your sellers how those questions went and what they were able to get out of their conversations by asking these F.A.C.T. based questions.

- Ensure every committed deal has a clear time frame, budget process, decision-making process, and next steps to take the conversation forward to winning the deal.

- Use your team at team meetings or stand ups to share best practices and lessons learned.

- Build Cheat Sheets for each letter in the F.A.C.T. Discovery Process, so that your team has the best questions for their buyers. They should be tied to your products and with your industry specifics, so that sellers are prepared for each call.

TACTIC #7
—Creating and Using a Business Case to Drive the Sale Forward

A tactic that can't be ignored is the ability to create and drive forward a compelling business case—one that leaves a buyer with practically no choice but to work with you because the impact and urgency you have conveyed to them is just so clear.

Developing that business case will draw upon the business drivers and needs you have identified for the buyer throughout the discovery process, drawing on some of the tools and capabilities we have highlighted earlier, synthesizing key learning from your sales materials, success stories, and pricing to close the deal.

In following up with a buyer to advance your case for a business deal, you may consider using an email template like the example below—not necessarily a carbon copy of this approach, but one that draws on some of the key points and methods used here:

> *Hi X,*
>
> *Thanks again for joining me on the live demo. As mentioned, I wanted to provide you with a pricing quote, as well as reiterate some of the value ACME can provide your organization. During our earlier conversations, you described **insert one to three critical technical, personal, or business pain points** as struggles you're experiencing with your current data and workflows. Below are some of the ways ACME has alleviated these issues for our customers and can help your company too:*
>
> *(Choose four to six from list below.)*

- **Leverage Data**—*We are an all-in-one e-commerce platform that provides brands one partner with all the data, tools, and services you need to grow your business. We have the ability to measure the market in real time, so you can scale your sales across all major e-commerce retailers (Amazon, Walmart, Target, etc.)*

- **Increase Speed for e-commerce results**—*ACME knows how to target your audience at every touchpoint across your media, paid search, remarketing, and even SEO to engage shoppers and drive higher conversion with content creation, content monitoring, pricing and promotions, inventory management, and ratings or reviews.*

- **Optimize your Marketing**—*We have depth and breadth with the most sophisticated technology in the industry. With daily tracking on 500 million products combined with marketing intelligence technology of competitive advertising and marketing performance, so you have unmatched visibility into traffic sources and conversions across the entire marketplace of competitive performance (pricing, promotions, traffic, conversion, sales).*

- **Learn from the Success of Others Like You**—*Our engagement team will ensure you and your team are set up to instantly gain the value of the network.*

- **Quickly Integrate with Existing Systems**—*Plug ACME into your systems you are using today in fifteen business days.*

- **Pricing**—*Our competitive pricing models are set up to find the best match for your organization now and as you continue to grow. We will provide the best ROI and have many customers we can point you to so you can hear it from them directly.*

- **Innovation**—*we are creating what the market needs before they know it. You will see significant product releases from us this year to provide you, our customer, with more options to increase your traffic, conversions, sales, and brand loyalty.*

As you can see, this is so much more than just a data tool. Our solutions are designed to help you be as efficient as possible and to maximize results, increase your market share, and make decisions based on seeing all the data. As we discussed, **insert closing comment with concrete next steps**. Please feel free to reach out any time you have questions.

Thanks,

...

As you can see in this example, we are leveraging past conversations from the F.A.C.T. Discovery Process to demonstrate that we understand the client needs, along with proof points that we can meet their requirements, such as product demos or trials.

A few key points to remember about building an effective business case:

- The process is exemplified by the idea of planting a seed— one that tells them they need to buy our services because we offer the best solution available on the market. Remember how I defined value as being able to help buyers solve their challenges better than anyone else out there.

- Fundamentally, our job is to make it explicit that we offer the best return on investment—not only investment in terms of dollars, but in terms of the energy and resources they invest—a precious allotment of their limited time. They may be spending more money on the solution we're offering, but they're also gaining other benefits, like reducing customer churn or employee turnover.

- Building a robust business case allows the buyer to bring in the necessary members of their team for making and driving decisions who are all hearing a consistent message on a few key points. Use the words and phrases you heard from the customer.

- At this stage of discussion, we've already undergone our discovery process and asked many commitment-level questions in order to identify the buyer's pain points and what they're seeking to improve. Whether it's tackling attrition or growth issues, bring specifics to discussing how your track record is directly appliable to the challenges the buyer faces.

- If you have a solid return on investment, then obviously add that to your business case. Fill in their specific data for this. You can also use cases or customer success stories to help validate the ROI.

- Review the business case in a discussion with your champion. Make this a business case that you both have input in creating. It gives them buy-in but also helps them use it internally.

Lastly, let's review what we do with this business case. Using the example email above, I would never send pricing without the content of that email. You should never send over just pricing or a proposal. When you send a pricing proposal, it will be forwarded to an executive, CFO, legal team, or others in the organization, so sell strong and outsell the competition.

Professional sellers want to drive the sales, so they highlight the pain (the stronger the pain the better). Then everyone who reads it understands *the reason why* they need to spend this money.

You must highlight your value add so people understand why they need to change with your product or services. Then you add in the concrete next steps to make sure that everyone is in the loop on how and when we are moving forward.

Suggested Rep Action Plan

- Prioritize building an effective business case that highlights the client's needs (not surface level) and how you can help them solve those needs better than anyone else.

- Tailor your business case to the unique needs of your customer, rather than adopting a cookie-cutter approach.

- Create a template to use. For example, I have a template for all my proposals where I fill in the company pain and have a list of my offerings (I delete the ones that do not apply to the scenario, but they are in my master template, so I never have to write them out again).

- Assume your business case will be shared to many contacts, so think of how your unique value add solves the collective business needs.

Suggested Manager Action Plan

- Require rookie sales professionals to demonstrate their ability to develop a robust business case and have them walk you through it in detail.

- Ensure your team always includes you on the business case, so you can see how your team best:

    o highlights the deep customer pain points
    o ties those pains to what we provide that is of unique value
    o leverages valid ROIs, customer success stories, analyst reports, white papers, etc. to validate and prove you can meet those needs

TACTIC #8
—Gaining Commitment on Budget, Timing, and Decision-Making Process

What are the main areas you will want your customers to commit to? The easy answer is the commitment to buy. But in many professional selling engagements today, that is at the very end of the process. So we need to know where we want to earn and gain customer commitment throughout the sales process.

Hopefully you can tell by now that I love to provide tools and cheat sheets, so here is another one. For a sales pro to close a deal and finally gain that all-important commitment, it's critical that they can answer five questions for themselves:

1. What's the "why" of this deal from the client perspective? What is their compelling event, pain, need, or reason for buying? Make sure the need is not surface level.

2. How have you uniquely positioned yourself to solve that client's needs better than anyone else? Based on the needs identified, have you communicated value that others cannot provide?

3. Where are you in winning this deal? Listen for buying signals as well as the potential pitfalls. How is the buyer working with you compared to your competition? Sell smarter by helping your buyer build the business case, ROI, Proof of Concept (POC), success criteria, etc.

4. What are the next steps to get to the close? Listen for the next steps the buyer is taking. The more the client has actions to take in the process the better. Overlay your

active involvement with executive summaries and mutual success plans to keep a timeline and mutual commitment.

5. How connected are you to all buyers? It is not just the business/department level decision maker you need to get commitment from. Ensure that you are working with the economic, legal, IT/Security, or the exec committee as well to get their approval and commitment to move forward.

Sealing the deal will often require obtaining approval from a range of decision makers throughout the sales process. You may want to make a checklist of the various points of contact that you'll need to win over.

- **IT/Security**—The internal IT "powers that be" have reviewed, certified, and approved moving forward as needed.

- **Legal**—Legal negotiations have taken place with red-lines and an agreed upon contract has been drafted for signature.

- **Economic Signer**—Final approver of the project has been identified and has approved the purchase.

- **Implementation Point of Contact**—The main point of contact to start implementation has been identified and is ready to move forward.

- **Business Decision Maker**—The main point of contact who wants this software. Budget might need to be established in department budget.

- **Executive Decision Maker**—C-level executive or board member approval might be needed.

Come prepared to answer those questions. It's wise to select two to three budget commitment questions that can help you cut to the heart of their potential concerns.

- "Can we talk about budget? Where are we in the process? This is what makes sense to me."
- "Do you suppose that you could share that number or budget with me?"
- "Tom, is there any way you could give me an idea of how much we'll have to work with?"
- "What were you hoping that investment might be?"
- "Hey, in round numbers, can you share with me what you are planning on spending?"
- "Let's assume you think we have the best solution to match your needs, but we were the most expensive solution by an additional 10%. Would that bring our conversations to an end?"
- "When you look at the cost, do you look at what you currently spend in terms of time, resources, and energy too?"
- "Can we talk about the budget, the time, and the resources needed that would be necessary to fix the issue we've outlined today?"
- "Most of the time I work on a project like this, the total investment falls somewhere in the range of $200,000 to $250,000. Do you think the amount that you would have available to invest would fall within that range?"
- "When you look at what it is costing you today (quantify the pain), how do you factor that into your decision-making process?"

Suggested Rep Action Plan

- Put the client first and foremost in considering their perspective—what is their compelling reason to join you?

What pain point are you helping them address? Ensure they are committed to solving those pain points.

- Reverse-engineer the steps you need to take to get them to "yes"—listen carefully to the next steps the buyer is taking.

- Practice your tough commitment questions beforehand, so you know how you want to ask for the budget, get to key decision makers, or understand their ability to move forward.

Suggested Manager Action Plan

- Make it a point to convey to your team that gaining commitment on budget, timing, and decision-making is a crucial tactic to master.

- Don't leave them to figure it out on their own—help them benefit from the sum of your own experiences.

- Have your reps' Right Now contracts include key areas they need to gain commitment on for where they are "right now" in the sales process.

TACTIC #9
—Overcoming Objections

In today's market, many buyers are more discerning than ever. Your goal is to have convincing answers for the roadblocks standing between you and that sale.

Objections are a natural part of the process; so when you get them, do not feel too dejected—and keep in mind that objections do not necessarily reflect on your tactics as a salesperson. Remember that objections are not personal rejections that attack you as a person. They also do not attack your character or your values.

On the contrary, objections are simply concerns and thoughts. It's healthy for them to be weighed, aired, and discussed. It's your job to help your prospect overcome these concerns and see the benefits of moving forward.

So, do not be afraid of receiving objections; embrace them as challenges, not as existential threats. By maintaining an objective view, sellers can take the emotion out of the equation and start to think of objections as ways to partner with the client to determine a way to go forward that is mutually beneficial.

Take it from me: rarely do objections reach the point of completely stopping the sales process.

Objections are not to be feared. They are to be embraced. Sometimes an objection is not an objection at all; sometimes it is just the client talking out loud. Some objections are even buying signals from buyers!

To start, we must understand the issue at hand that we are trying to overcome. Sometimes they are obvious, like a momentary obstacle of not having any room in the budget.

When faced with a roadblock, most sellers are ready to talk about the value of their product and the ROI it will provide. They have evidence and buyer success stories to prove why the buyer should go forward. And sometimes those tactics work great.

The key is to simply not be caught off guard. Be ready for these objections and plan to address them. Practice scenarios in advance, and you will never be thrown for a loop at the concerns a client presents to you.

As we discussed in our chapter on mental preparation, we should make it a point to ask ourselves, before every call, to think about the obstacles, roadblocks, hurdles, and objections you might encounter that could potentially impede your sales progress.

The good news is that in each and every stage—from prospecting, to discovery, to prove/demo, to negotiation, to close—there are probably only three or four objections you will deal with in the vast majority of cases. Yes, there can always be a concern raised completely out of left field. But being prepared for the most common objections is the most important thing you can do.

Plan for those situations that make up the vast majority of objections and have a great pitch ready. Proactively address the concerns head on when you can. Be ready for objection as well, enabling you to produce a solid and fluid answer that you have practiced with confidence.

Let's get down to the most important details. I will provide a three-step process and five tactics for overcoming objections in the second step.

There are two basic steps to the process of overcoming objections:

#1: Listen by Giving Acknowledgement

Be an active listener. This is the first requirement for a sales professional to build trust. How often are you going to place your trust in someone who barely seems to be registering what you tell them, only waiting for their turn in the conversation to speak?

Actively listening demonstrates to your buyer that you are interested in their concern and actually care what they have to say. It also helps you to frame your response well, using the proper tactics.

Using these tactics in buyer conversations can take time to get accustomed to. It's not always intuitive to be persistent or press on when you hear a "no." But when someone tells you something negative, a rejection, or something that stands in the way of getting what you want, you must change the dynamic to move forward. Otherwise you will have a difficult time advancing in sales.

The best way to start overcoming an objection is to actively listen and acknowledge their perspective. Don't just make them feel heard—actually *hear* them. Take in what they're telling you. Put yourself in their shoes. Think of all the potential risks and considerations rattling around in their brains.

And you should acknowledge the points that arise. After all, acknowledging does not mean agreement. Far from it. Acknowledging does not mean accepting what they are saying. It means hearing them and letting them know they were heard with phrases like:

- "I hear you. . . " (without a "but")
- "Thank you for telling me that. . . "
- "I appreciate your perspective. . . "
- "I hear you. . . please go on. . . "

- "I hear that often, but I hate making assumptions about what that means to you. Can you please tell me more?"
- "That makes sense. . . "
- "Interesting. . . "
- Laugh at what they say like you get it
- Nod your head
- "Let me repeat that back to you, so I can make sure I heard you correctly. You said. . . "

Where does that leave us?

On the path to building a real relationship. Starting here helps build a sense of credibility and trust. It also reframes how the buyers sees you, your product, or your capabilities. This is how we develop rapport and build our relationships with clients.

#2: Understand and Reply

Your client's trust in you can be directly correlated with how much they think you understand where they are coming from.

And I do not mean understand on a surface level. We need to really understand what the hurdle is that we are trying to overcome versus just responding because it's part of a sales script that we have committed to memory to get to our revenue goal.

Get to the heart of the objection. This is where asking questions is such a powerful tool for helping you to drill in on the heart of their concern.

Sometimes as you ask questions, you may find that the reason they have stated up front has more below the surface. Maybe it's not so much a matter of "there's no room in the budget" as much as it's a matter of "we're worried about getting our lunch eaten by some new app a kid invented in the next quarter."

Perhaps the real concern has less to do with today's bottom-line and their appetite for risk versus innovation or their fears about where the business trends are headed in their industry.

In short, the concern may not be what the buyer originally told you. Sometimes they are not even able to fully articulate what the problem is—they just know they have an alarm bell going off somewhere, or they worry that they're going to be left holding the bag if you can't deliver what you promised. As sellers, we must be comfortable and confident in our replies to keep as much control as possible in the sales process.

There are five tactics to overcoming objections that will help you understand and reply in the most effective way possible.

Tactic 1: Dig In

Strong sellers put the conversation back on the buyer to give additional details or concerns to know the root issues. This is the best time to ask a question!

Ask permission to explore and understand the issue. No, you don't have all the time in the world in most meetings, but you can request time up front to ensure that you both have a shared understanding of the environment they are operating within.

Restate the concern as you see it. Maybe your wording and reframing will bring a different perception to the table and the buyer will see the concept more clearly.

In short, embrace the objections instead of trying to defeat them.

Here's an example:

Your prospect says: "Does your product do. . .?"

Your reply: *"Yes, but before I go into too much detail, what are you looking to achieve? How are you handling it now?"*

Or you might try:

"It does, but before I go into too much detail, why do you ask? Is there a specific issue you have today that is important to you that you want to discuss?"

Your prospect says: "My biggest challenge/need/concern is. . . (I am not sure my team will want to learn a new process.)"

Your seller: *"I can understand how that could be a challenge. What have you done so far to try to address it?"*

Your prospect does not commit or gives ambiguous answers.

While most people do not see this as an objection, it 100% stalls you from moving forward. Objections are not always about responding to what is said but also how to respond to what is not said.

Your reply: *"Assume this was something you wanted; how would you envision going forward?"*

Your prospect: "I am not sure if you can solve this for us."

Your reply: *"Thanks for the honesty. I appreciate that. Can you go into more detail and tell me why you say that? Let's start with how you are solving for that issue today?"*

Tactic 2: Brutal Honesty

Contrary to what many seem to believe, a seller *can* be nice and professional without being a pushover and just agreeing to whatever the buyer says.

We can all tell when we are telling people what they want to hear versus the actual truth. So, address the tough issues head on!

Be blunt in your response. Here's a little tip you'll remember from *Mary Poppins:* "A spoonful of sugar makes the medicine go down."

You may find that you can be quite straightforward in the content of the message you deliver if you simply watch *how* you say it.

Maintain a calm tonality that removes any sarcasm, so you do not offend. That is the value of complete honesty. The best place to use this is in difficult or ambiguous situations.

Buyers are conditioned to salespeople telling them what they think they want to hear. So they will be quite pleasantly surprised with straight-up honesty. Face the interaction differently and disrupt the pattern to give a reply the prospect is not expecting.

Your prospective client has probably been pitched to by your competition or another seller trying to sell them something. So they are conditioned to not answer cold calls, not reply to cold emails, or to push them away should they get through.

And let's be realistic, cold calling and prospecting for new business is one of the hardest sales tactics to do effectively. You have lots of rejection, limited time, and buyer attention span.

This brutal honesty tactic works well in this very difficult environment.

Here are some examples:

Your prospect says, "Send me your information."

Your reply: "*Typically when I do that, it ends up lost in a folder or in the trashcan. Is it fair for me to assume that's the case? Can I get three minutes to tell you why others in your role/vertical have wanted to see and hear more from me? After that time, if you do not think I am providing value, then we can end the conversation.*"

or

"*I can do that, but typically people just delete it. And that does not help anyone. Is that the case here? Or can I get two minutes to see what type of info you might want as it might help me provide you with something that is actually valuable and needed?*"

Your prospect says, "We will think about it and get back to you."

Your reply: "*Typically when I hear someone say they will get back to me, it really means they are not sure this is something they want to do. They just might not want to tell me NO. Is it fair for me to assume that's the case? Or can I get three minutes to tell you why others in your role/vertical have wanted to see and hear more from me? After that time, if you do not think I am providing value, then we can end the conversation.*"

Your prospect says, "Give me a call back in two weeks."

Your reply: "*Typically when I hear that, it is just a way for people to get me off the phone, and this is not a need. Is it fair for me to assume that's the case? Or can I get ten minutes to really talk with you and see if this is something you might want?*"

Your prospect says, "I'm too busy," or "It's bad timing."

Your reply: "*I hear that often, as people typically do not want to take sales calls. With that said, there are a few key items that make us completely unique and a must-have for businesses like yours. I know learning about options and knowing critical vendors is important, so you know what is available to you when you need it. I would hate for you to miss this opportunity to learn. So where do we go from here?*"

Tactic 3: Take Away

This tactic puts a role reversal where you get the client to become the seller. This is best used after enough pain is identified or a unique value has been provided.

Take away the client's ability to move forward and get them to tell you why they need your product or service. This gives them an opportunity to verbally validate what they heard, liked, and found to be the most impactful for their business.

Create a role reversal to see how the buyer sells you.

Here are some examples:

You find yourself at the end of a meeting to get buyer commitment to move forward.

Your statement: *"Based on what I've heard so far, Mr. Prospect, it sounds like you have some needs. But my sense is that they're probably not important enough to justify taking a closer look at our solution. Is that a fair statement?"*

or:

"Based on what I've heard so far, Mr. Prospect, it sounds like you have some needs. But I am getting the sense that this is not the right time for you to move forward. Is that a fair statement?"

You are in a pricing discussion where the client thinks your price is high.

Your statement: *"Assuming you came to believe that we had the best solution, but you found yourself looking at an investment of about $250,000, would that bring our discussion to an end?"*

Here is a special note on when we talk about investments or costs with customers: most people tend to think of an investment as just the cost for the product or service. But in truth, it is much more than that.

Think of the total investment they have now and with you in terms of dollars, time, resources, effort, heartache, risk of not changing, internal reputation, employee satisfaction, and retention of buyers and employees. And think of the opportunity cost to them as you continue to go on building a relationship and partnership. All those factors have an impact on cost.

Tactic #4: Play Naïve

One of the best things about a seller starting to sell a new product or joining a new company is that—to be blunt—they do not know anything.

They do not know the details of what the product does. They don't know how it works; they don't know what is involved with it. They do not know any details on how to sell with its unique value, what it means to different buyer personas, or how to engage clients in a meaningful way.

There's a lot to learn, clearly. So, what do new sellers do to figure it out? They ask a lot of basic questions. They slow the process down to get the baseline information. They do this to get to the point of absolute clarity!

The same principle applies here with playing naïve. Using this tactic gets the seller to purposely struggle and ask basic questions, so the prospect has to give you additional details. The tonality used in this tactic is inquisitive and the pace is slower, so they show they need help from the buyer. You might have never thought about the importance of voice tonality until now, but it's essential for a seller.

Some examples:

Your prospect says, "It is costing me way too much."

Your reply: *"When you say it is costing you too much. . . what does that mean?"*

or:

"I hear you. So I do not make an assumption, can you tell me what that means?"

or:

"When you say it is costing you too much, are you thinking about just the initial cost? Or the cost associated with the time, effort, resources, and internal results you are getting today? So, when you look at cost. . . what does that mean?"

Go back to our special note that an investment or cost does not just mean dollars. While you can still display an understanding of how costs impact the business differently, we play naïve to get the buyer to defend the objection and tell us the details.

This tactic also works great when you are trying to get a decision out of a buyer that is not committing to a decision. You could ask:

"Where do we go from here?"

or:

"How do we get from where we are now to where you are comfortable saying, 'Let's do it!' or 'Let's not do it?'"

Your prospect says, "Send me your pricing, and I will get my boss to approve it."

Your reply: *"What does getting approval mean?"*

Your prospect says, "Does your product do. . .?" (with lots of follow up questions)

Your reply: *"You are going down a very specific path with lots of questions. Is there something that's critical to your business that we aren't addressing?"*

Tactic #5: Be the One Who Messes Up

I'm sure you've often heard the old maxim, "The buyer is always right?"

While I do not agree with that phrase, I do agree that the perception of the buyer being correct helps overcome difficult situations.

Sellers typically avoid conflict as they do not want to piss off the buyer by holding them accountable.

When using this tactic, the seller intentionally "falls on the sword" to make it easy for the prospect to feel okay. How do sellers do this? Use phrases like: *"Did I miss the mark?"* *"Did I make an error?"* or *"I completely messed this up and want to make sure I do not make the same mistake again so. . ."*

Some examples to keep in mind:

Your prospect says, "Your price seems high"

Your reply: *"Pablo, I sense that you're not 100% comfortable with my proposal. I thought I demonstrated the value and ROI you could get, but I must have done a horrible job. I am sorry if I didn't. Have I missed the mark on what we are solving and the value to your business?"*

Here is another common scenario: your prospect missed a meeting, deadline, or action.

Your statement: *"Danielle, I'm confused. My understanding was that I was going to hear from you today. Did I write down the wrong date?"*

Your prospect will not commit or is being ambiguous in their answers.

Your reply: *"Elaine, I recently got off a call where I upset a buyer. I would hate to make the same mistake here, so I want to ensure I have a clear understanding of what you need to move forward. Can you please tell me. . ."*

Move On

The final step is to move on. Sometimes you've done all you can.

Most sellers want to "beat" the objection and get the buyer to agree to it. But doing that makes a winner and a loser in the process.

There is no need to rub it in your client's face, so if we used a tactic that got the buyer to acknowledge there is not an issue or you changed their perspective where they no longer raise it as a concern, you have already received confirmation. Move on. Do not look back or even bring it up.

For those objections where you want to ensure the customer is ready to move on, use one of these phrases to get a *yes* or *no* back.

Before you ask the direct questions, make sure you follow Step 1 with acknowledging the buyer and Step 2 where you responded with value. This way, you can overcome the objection with:

- *"Have I addressed all of your concerns today on that issue, so I know you are committed to move forward?"*
- *"Has everything I've discussed made sense to you?"*
- *"Can we move forward or is there something else you wish to discuss?"*

As you continue to get better and better at using these tactics, two things should start to develop.

1. You will be able to combine these tactics together. As you get more comfortable in the arena and begin to put more of the puzzle pieces together, it really gets fun to engage with clients. Here are some more examples. See if you can spot the combination of tactics used.

   a. *"I would hate to misunderstand you. Can you tell me what 'that' means to you?"* Tactics used are Be the One that Messes Up followed by Playing Naïve.

   b. *"I know you said that you think you do not have a need, but I also heard you state earlier that you are concerned with. . . (enter pain point). I am curious to know what you have done to solve that and why it is not working the way you want?"* Tactics used are Take Away followed by a Dig In.

2. You can start to proactively overcome the objections. Take an objection in the very early stage of prospecting when you typically hear a client say, "This will not work for us," or "It is not really a need of ours." Ask yourself, "What is the way to proactively overcome that?"

   Since we know it is early in our sales process, and since we have already reviewed our G.O.L.D. Elevator Pitch Process, we can use the "L" statement to proactively overcome objections.

Here is an example where I will use the O, L, and D portion of G.O.L.D. with the key phrase I am referring to in bold.

"I have talked with thousands of sales leaders in my day (that's the O in G.O.L.D.) *and **often I hear that they do not have a need or are not sure if what I offer works for them,** but as we continue to talk, they tell me they are struggling to get sellers ramped up quickly, are concerned they will not hit their quotas that continue to rise, and are overwhelmed with all the nuances of coaching that need to happen on their team to increase results* (the L).

What would it mean to you and the impact to your business if I was able to help in these areas?

Is it worth another fifteen minutes in our conversation to see if I could help in ways you have not thought about yet?" (the D).

Here's a concrete example: I want to share a story about a seller I trained in 2017 in Toronto. (I'm talking to you, Rory M.!) He leveraged all these tactics at one time or another, but one in particular became his signature go-to. He loved to be the one that messed up.

He was constantly telling buyers how he messed up, missed the mark, must have totally missed what the client wanted, wrote down the wrong next step (even though he didn't), etc.

It went in the face of so much of what we know or think we know about the working world, in which we convince ourselves that we have to act like we have the answers all of the time or that we are incapable of screwing up.

Not Rory. He paddled in the exact other direction. He eagerly took the blame every time the buyer stalled—surely, he must have messed up on the date. Surely, it was his fault that they couldn't find the attachment. And since he did not want to do it again, he vowed to make sure items going forward were more detailed throughout.

He even did this on pricing. Sometimes the buyer would point out that Rory had presented a price that was demonstrably higher than the competition.

When the client would point this out, Rory would say something to the effect of, *"I know I broke down the problems you want to solve and how we do it. We even discussed the impact it has on your business. I thought I did that well and you wanted to move forward with me. Sorry if I completely messed things up. Does the initial cost being too high kill this opportunity for both of us?"*

To finish off this chapter, here's a cheat sheet to help you quickly see how you can create a one-pager for yourself to be effective with overcoming objections.

I build these for my buyers all the time, and people hang them on their walls or use them as a reference to prep for meetings, use during meetings, or to evaluate their effectiveness post meetings.

Overcoming Objections cheat sheets: The tactics and the objections with answers.

Tactic	Definition	Example
Dig In	Put the conversation back on the customer to give additional details or concerns to know the root issues. Best time to ask a Question!	**Prospect:** "I am not sure if you can solve this for us." **You:** "Thanks for the honesty. I appreciate that. Can you go into more details and tell me why you say that…let's start with how you are solving for that issue today?"
Brutal Honesty	Use in difficult or ambiguous situations. Face it differently and disrupt the pattern to give a reply the prospect is not expecting.	**Prospect:** "Send me your info." **You:** "I can do that and typically people just delete it when I do that, that does not help anyone. Is that the case here or can I get 2 minutes to see what type of info you might want as it might help?"
Take Away	Use after enough pain identified or unique value has been provided. Create a role reversal to see how the customer sells you.	**You:** "Based on what I have heard, it sounds like you have a need. But I am getting the sense that this is not the right time for you to move forward. Is that a fair statement?"
Be Naïve	Purposely struggle and ask for additional details so the prospect has to give you additional details.	**Prospect:** "That is way more than we need." **You:** "I hear you. So, I do not make an assumption, can you tell me what that means?"
Be the one who messed up	Intentionally "Fall on the sword" and make it easy for the prospect to feel OK.	**You:** "I am getting the sense you are not happy with the information I sent you. Did I completely miss the mark on what I sent you?"

Objection	Typical Sales Stage	Tactic	Example Response
I am not the Decision Maker	Prospecting or Opportunity	Play Naïve	"But you are involved in helping the business …right?"
No budget/price too high	Opportunity - Proposal	Dig In	"So how do you look at cost vs. lost opportunities?" Or "If you increased revenues and advertising effectiveness, how does that factor into the price discussion?"
Too Busy/no time/bad timing/not a priority right now/other priorities/ can't get it approved	Prospecting or Opportunity	Brutal Honesty	"I hear that often as people typically do not want to take sales calls. With that said, there are a few key items that make us completely unique and a must have for businesses liked yours. I know learning about options and knowing critical vendors is important, so you know what is available to you when you need it. I would hate for you to miss this opportunity to learn. So where do we go from here?"

Objection	Typical Sales Stage	Tactic	Example Response
Won't work for us (tried this before, not ready for it, not sure what we want, etc.)	Prospecting or Opportunity	Be the one who messed up	"Thank you for telling me. I must have completely misunderstood what you are trying to do."
Everything in lock down (not investing, not doing new projects)	Prospecting – Demo	Dig in	"So, let's look at options. What are you doing today, how is it working and what are the main things you want to improve?"
We need to do a Trial First	Proposal or Trial	Dig In	"Got it. What are you hoping to accomplish in that trial?"

Suggested Rep Action Plan

- Earlier in the chapter we talked about practice, as in practicing your responses as well as your sales pitch. Practice the potential objections you may hear in the meeting that the client might raise. Think outside the box and challenge yourself with how you want to answer.

- What are the most common objections you get in each stage of the sales process? Write down two or three objections you get in each stage and then a few tactics with the replies for each objection.

- Test it out by saying it out loud to yourself, and then to your teammates and managers. Then do it with buyers. If you pick a week where every day you take a sales stage and determine those two or three objections per stage, then you can have your cheat sheet in one week.

- You can overcome significant hurdles now, so what are you waiting for?

Suggested Manager Action Plan

Overcoming objections is one of my favorite topics as the objections never get old and our replies need to be constantly rehearsed. Here are some great ways to do exactly that:

1. In pre-call prep, ask the seller what objections they might get. Then have them reply to you with how they would handle them. If the replies are good, validate them and move on. If it needs work, then coach.

2. Bring those above examples into a team meeting and review them as a team. Review successes and lessons learned from other teammates.

3. Do a "huddle" or "stand up" meeting to review sales scripts for fifteen minutes. Give up to three objections in rapid fire and pick a seller to respond. In this time, you should be able to hit seven to twelve objections and replies. Validate what worked well, coach what needs improvement, and keep pushing your team until they can demonstrate how to execute properly!

Tactic #10
—Give Yourself a Raise by Creating a Strong Referral Program

What seller does not want to make more money?

While earning more money may not necessarily be your number one driver, depending on your focus and stage in life, it is definitely important to most sellers. So, let's be sure to work on a tactic that directly impacts our wallet.

Any seller that wants a raise, here is the best way to give yourself a 25% pay increase this year!

I often talk with sales sellers, and they love referrals. They say it is one of the best ways to grow their business, as those sales tend to be sold quicker and for higher value.

Sadly, sellers often do not have a plan to get referrals. And if they do, they are not strong enough to leverage the different types of referrals they can ask for and use to help close future sales.

Let's break down what is involved with a having a strong referral program.

Different Types of Referrals to Ask For

There are multiple types of referrals and references you can ask for. With social networks today and all the online connections available at your fingertips, there are a ton of opportunities to ask for referrals.

- Direct referral to another contact at the same company. This is critically important as you continue to engage the multiple decision makers and buying decision processes that are involved in sales today, especially B2B sales. Ask for them by name, title, or department.

- Direct referral to another contact at a different company. You must think beyond the current company. Look at their history to know how long they have been at their current company or previous companies. They might have a significant number of contacts at other companies that you might be targeting.

- Referral to an industry or network group. This is where a seller needs to take ten seconds out of their day to look at the background of their contact to determine if there are areas you might want to get an additional contact. Open your mind to go beyond the obvious scope of an industry or LinkedIn Group. It might be a contact from their past professional organizations, religious organizations, community organizations, schools, location, role, etc.

- Endorsements of any kind. These can be five-star reviews, recommendations, quotes, case studies. You can put these on your LinkedIn profile as a recommendation, attach the positive review to your business, or add the reference or quote to your auto signature or presentation materials.

- Use referrals throughout each step of your sales process. A great example is using that referral as a reference for potential future business with a prospect you are going after. You can leverage your expertise in selling to specific industries and personas, or even to solve specific business challenges. As the saying goes, "People buy from people." That's why it's so crucial to understand the persona of the kind of people you intend to persuade.

When to Ask for Referrals

There is no need to wait until after the buyer buys, or even three, six, or twelve months later. A simple rule to follow is to ask after a positive conversation with the buyer.

If you solved a problem, gave them value, proved to be an industry or product expert, established rapport, made them laugh, or got any form of commitment from the contact in your last conversation, then you have every right to ask for a referral.

Typically, I encourage sellers to ask for referrals during some of these times:

- at the close of any call where the client is excited to move forward or sees value in the product, service, company, or me
- two to four weeks post close to have a checkup call stating, "Wanted to check in and see how things are going and ask. . ."
- two weeks post launch
- two weeks post renewal
- at the end of positive engagement

Anyone that touches the buyer and has a positive engagement should be asking for referrals.

Think of all the touchpoints we have with our buyers. It's such a missed opportunity to let one of those chances go when testimonials and referrals will always be one of the most powerful tools you can harness for attracting future clients and business.

For example, let's say that you just completed a quarterly business review, closed a support ticket, reviewed a product enhancement, received a positive net promoter score, have a high "buyer health score," or even hosted a buyer event like a client advisory board or annual buyer summit. While you're basking in the glow of victory, don't miss the opportunity to ask for a testimonial, referral, or endorsement!

I have even seen this work well after a cold call or when a client does not buy, believe it or not. I have seen executive sponsors ask other executives as well.

Do not close your own doors by only asking after you close a deal.

How to Ask for a Referral

Almost every time I roleplay with sellers to review how they ask for a referral, I get the basic reply of, "Do you know of anyone that you could refer me to, so I might be able to help them like I helped you?"

While it is asking for a referral, it is the bare minimum.

Here is what a strong referral program sounds like:

- "Thank you for your time today. I appreciate you being actively involved in the discussion. Before we go, can you please refer me to three contacts that might be in need of our solution?" Go big and ask for more than one. The more you helped them or provided those positive experiences we discussed, the more confident you should be in your ask.

- If you ask for three and did not get them, then a buyer will usually feel bad. Save them from that feeling and keep it positive as you have many other options. For example, "Thanks for the referral, can I get. . .

  - . . . a LinkedIn reference?"
  - . . . a buyer testimonial?"

o I noticed you are connected to. . . would you introduce me to. . .?"

o When I need a buyer reference, would you mind if I connected you to buyers that want to hear from other buyers?"

When to Use Those Referrals

Now that we have the referrals, we must use them throughout the entire sales process. Maximize every opportunity as you interact with buyers. Those can include:

- Initial touchpoint. Whether you meet them in a cold call, tradeshow, or wherever you start the sale process, referrals at this stage help you build trust and make the contact more willing to listen. Referrals at this stage create curiosity and develop interest about you, your company, your solution, and the problems you solve. A great example is to use "referred" in your email subject line/cold call, as it will significantly increase your response rates. I have seen over a 5X increase in response rates from sellers using this tactic. The higher up the corporate ladder, the higher your response rate will go.

- As you learn who is involved in the sales process, referrals help identify all the stakeholders and gain access to decision makers.

- As your solution is being vetted, referrals help you overcome objections and position yourself against the competition.

- As you negotiate toward a close, a reference from an existing buyer will help you gain agreement on that deal you are trying to close.

Suggested Rep Action Plan

- As you close a sale, set a calendar reminder four weeks out and twelve weeks out from the close date (adjust as needed if longer than a month's implementation time).

  - Four weeks post close—check in call with the key decision makers, users, and influencers. Yep, that's right—check *all* the key contacts! Even if implementation is rocky, make the call. Hear them out, offer assistance, validate their business decision by reminding them why they bought and the pain relief they will get from your solution. Let them know you care and are here for them.

  - Twelve weeks post close—ask for the referral. And ask with confidence! Ask for three referrals that they can directly introduce you to at different companies. You might be asking, "Why three?" Well, think about it; you might be following up with the buyer post-sale close. That sends a clear message that you care about them and are ensuring that your solutions bring them the value they wanted. All these behaviors signal that you have high credibility and have given them more than they would likely come to expect from the average seller. It's a simple rule of thumb: if you give more, then *ask* for more. Then if they only give you one, they feel badly and are willing to do more for you. Then you can ask for additional items like:

    - A specific connection you want. . . they are not going to look at their connections from their LinkedIn profile and dig around looking for the perfect person to connect with you. That's YOUR job. You are going to be the one doing that research and making the "ask" to them as targeted, clear, and specific as possible. Examples could be a connection from a past company they worked at or a connection they have at a company you want to target.

- A LinkedIn reference that you can post on your profile—highlighting you, your product and/or your company (you can even write it for them—everyone is at a shortage of time and will appreciate any support you can give in making an ask as easy on them as possible).

- A case study or quote you can use for marketing materials or as a tag line on your auto signature.

- A reference for you for potential new clients.

o Just do it. When you close that deal, set your reminders and stick to those reminders once they come up!

- Give yourself a weekly goal. For example, I will get two referrals each week. Remember to ask other buyer-facing roles to be your referral advocates too.

- Set calendar reminders for you to ensure you follow your action plan. Use the reminders until it becomes part of your process that you do EVERY TIME!

Suggested Manager Action Plan

- In your first team meeting of each month, go through your closed deals from the prior month and make sure everyone has their calendar appointments.

- Remind your team to ask for three referrals—and clarify for them the different types of referrals they can get, so they cast a wide enough net.

- Get involved with the follow-up. . . you can help with the four-week post-sale call too, especially if there is an issue.

- Share the success with your team and your peers. I have seen many companies put a referral field in their salesforce automation system (e.g., Salesforce.com or HubSpot), so they can track the quantity and impact of the referrals to their bookings.

- Track referrals brought in by your team.

- Set clear expectations for the number of referrals you expect to see each quarter and hold your team accountable.

BONUS TACTICS
—For Unique Seller Situations

The ten tactics we have explored will be powerful tools for any sales pro or manager's tool kit. But there are also a variety of other situations that can arise, so here is a little bonus. Knowing there are some large, unique factors to different professional selling processes, I wanted to give you five bonus tactics.

BONUS TACTIC #1
—Partner/Channel Sales

It's critical to understand that partner/channel sales are a very different beast from direct sales. Let's level the set with some clarification—what exactly is a channel partner?

Channels or channel partners can do many things for sellers. They provide us leads, bring us into deals, give us access to inventory or services, or implement our products as strategic integrator. They can be niche players or broad. But in most cases, they are involved in the sales process.

So, let's start with understanding the types of resellers and why it is a mutually beneficial relationship.

- Lead generator—hand you leads for a referral fee.
- Help you sell—they have the product, the technology, the infrastructure, the relationships, the customer eyeballs, the expertise, etc. Some have a great relationship with your key decision maker. They increase your value—so in turn you need to share in the value and buy from them or provide some commission (or double pay commissions). Some common channel partners are:

  - Distributor—they can have the product.
  - Corporate Reseller or value-added reseller where you can use their "paper" to get deals through with less contractual or legal obstacles.
  - Branded direct.
  - Manufacturer direct—might only provide part of the solution.

- o Internet retailer like Amazon US, Amazon Canada, Walmart, Instacart, Chewy, etc. They have the eyeballs and can be a great avenue for you to sell your product.

- Help you integrate: professional services/strategic integrators—they get the professional services portion of the deal.

So, what is the goal of having channel partners?

There are several reasons why people use them.

- to instantly gain access to a sales force (ideally already trained in the product or technology, just need to know your specifics).
- to instantly gain access to customers (leveraging the partner's relationships).
- to increase ability, speed, or infrastructure to implement.

Keep in mind that there are some specific differences when selling through a channel in regard to the sales process, customer engagement, and deal management.

Since you might not be selling directly to the customer, selling through distribution/resellers is different. . . you need to:

- Find the right channel partners.
- Properly onboard them.
- Know how to work deals.
- Gain agreement on what the partnership is so we know who does what, when, and with what expectation.

How do you go about finding the right channel partner?

First, you need to have a targeted approach that is aligned on business strategy. Your strategy will dictate the items you need. For example, if I sell cyber security software solutions, I will look for partners that have strong relationships with chief information security officers (CISOs).

I know they know about my cyber security technologies and the needs that CISOs have.

So, at the surface, they seem like a good match. But I also know that I will not be their only partner, so I need to work with them to ensure our business strategies align. At a high level, you need to look at how these two businesses can have a balanced approach to drive business with mutual customer accounts. Look for:

- How do I match up with this partner to service customers in my territory? Is there a good mix of reps for me to leverage and engage with? Can we manage the relationship to provide the level of support needed, so we both can generate consistent business?

- What is their quality as it relates to their business scope, their experience, or their relationships?

- Getting past "hype" and getting clear commitments to and from the channel partner.

  - Executive level commitment with actions/access to the team.
  - Manager commitment to engage the team and support the efforts.
  - Rep level commitment with actions/access to their customers.

- Actions! Their actions are stronger than words.

- ○ What level of commitment are you looking for? Do you want to have a certain number of accounts you mutually target, leads per quarter they provide, new client introductions they make each month, etc.?
- ○ We need to see how they actively bring us into deals, help us navigate the customer buying process, and partner in a way to leverage our collective knowledge, skills, and options to most effectively work the deal.

- Ensure you can support them.

  - ○ Location—can you get to them often enough? Not that it must be face-to-face, but make sure you have the ability to work with them enough hours in the day to be effective.
  - ○ You need to provide materials to the partner, so they know how to position you, market your product, sell your product, or implement your product. That means you need to train them, arm them, and support them. Some technology or tools might be needed (e.g., a "partner portal" for lead submission and tracking, co-marketing materials, sales collateral, and product/technical training), so ensure it aligns with what your business strategy can provide for the foreseeable future.

With Channel Partners, you need to be proactive to align the business strategy. It takes some steps when you are onboarding and developing your sales force:

- Access to your partner portal/portal walk through. Show them what you are giving them and how it ties to their sales success, ability to make money, ability to provide their customers great products or services, etc. Show them how easy it is to submit leads and to get collateral like product one pagers, white papers, technical briefs, competitive advantages, presentation decks, access to systems to demo, etc.

- Training. You must make sure they understand all of the details needed to sell your product. Here is a list of items you need to consider when training on how to sell a product. Determine what pieces are relevant to your environment:

  o Product training

    ▪ Macro
      - History and market landscape.
      - Types of products and what our products solve.
      - Players in space.

    ▪ Micro
      - Product details—what we offer, what it is and is not.
      - Product example or demonstration.
      - Product activities—get them to use and feel it with live use cases, customer success stories, and hands-on access if possible.
      - Niche and nuances (e.g., integrations with systems like Oracle).
      - Specific product features and functionality.
      - Competitive landscape deep dive with our unique differentiation in the market.

- Customer feedback.
- Product road map.
- Stand alone or integration into product suite.

o Sales enablement training—now that they know the product, you must determine what they need to be able to sell the product. Think of the sales tactics you reviewed in this book. How would you want to arm your channel partner to sell in the most effective manner? The level of detail will vary according to how much the channel partner needs to sell without your involvement.

- Sales Tactics:
  - Messaging—you might even give them the G.O.L.D Elevator Pitch Process and some examples.
  - Unique value add tied to business needs.
  - Questions to ask.
  - Objections to overcome.

- Sales and Marketing materials
  - Marketing campaigns you are running, plan to run, or want to run in conjunction with the channel partner.
  - Marketing materials that are customer-facing, like pitch decks, or sales collateral, like product one pagers.
  - Demo script including demo environment.
  - Pricing.
  - Installation process.

- Cross functional team involvement.

- Sales action plan to drive business
  - Territory planning—align reps to reps to build the structure. This can be done off of location, industries, or verticals served.
  - Account mapping—reps look at their business relationships, leads, and current opportunities to figure out what to align on for new accounts to target, what accounts to pull each other in, and what current open opportunities to bring in and close.
  - Sales or technical certification—the more people know and understand your product, the more they will sell it, especially if they like it and see the value it provides. Get the team certified to sell and demonstrate your product to build that alignment.
  - Changes to compensation—for example, some companies will pay higher commission percentages if the channel partner receives certain certifications.
  - Have a consistent engagement strategy, so you ensure you are in front of your channel partners. This can be done in many ways, but the goal is to keep your product or service top of mind for your channel partner, so they are always thinking about you.
  - I recommend you engage and talk about deals and how to move them forward. In these "deal walkthrough"

conversations, you can continue to reinforce the training to arm your channel partners on your elevator pitch, qualification questions (qualify an opportunity), discovery questions (uncover needs, business impact, personal motivation to move), demo, case studies, pricing, contract/terms, common objections, etc.

- Most reps assume their channel partners know how to make sales, so they skip this level of engagement.

Also make sure you take a different approach when working with channel partners:

- Have a plan—territory alignment planning sessions or targeted customer outreach (i.e. account based marketing) that you want to do together.
- Have a cadence to interaction, get involved with deals, review deals and accounts, share thought leadership, tag them in posts on LinkedIn.
- Know reps and other key leadership, so you can leverage your relationships.

  o Who does what? Document it each time, so you do not forget who to turn to.
  o Share success stories. Highlight the rep you worked with to their leadership and talk about how you won the deal. You will be surprised by the referrals you get.

- Know the reps.

  o Are they strong sellers? If not, how do you support or guide them to get better?

- ○ Where do you need to get involved?
- ○ What do you trust? When do you push them to ensure you win the deal?

- DO NOT make assumptions on how they sell—ask, state, politely demand it.

    - ○ Understand their sales process and drive it if you can. Fill in any gaps with what you need to be a coach for them. An easy way to raise that is "one thing that worked great for me and another channel partner was. . ." or "can we take five minutes to look at this from another perspective? I have missed things before and lost deals that way. I like to learn from my past mistakes. Can we. . ."
    - ○ Take an active role in ensuring the selling skills we need to implement are being used.
    - ○ Get proof—"How has this customer bought from you before?"

Perhaps above all, it's critical to gain agreement on partner management:

- Goals and expectations—with plans, inspection, and mutual accountability on how you plan to mutually grow your businesses.

    - ○ Be clear on what each of you can do.
    - ○ Be fair—balance accountability versus hope.
    - ○ Be willing to give a little to get things back—you might have to prove yourself first.

Suggested Rep Action Plan

- Understand the various channel partners you'll work with and how you can develop win-win relationships based on mutual gain.

- Determine what type of channel partners are best for you to go after with what your business can properly support.

- Spend your time on the right channel partners who are engaging and working with you on deals and accounts.

Suggested Manager Action Plan

- Help your teams to understand the nuances with channel partners and the differences in working with them.

- Leverage your position to help drive activities and executive alignment at the channel partner.

- Help develop out the infrastructure, compensation, resources, tools, partner portals, etc. that will be needed for your channel partner program to be successful. I know we will always want more money, resources, and tools, but you must use what you have at the moment to be successful.

BONUS TACTIC #2
—Sales Demos

Of course, one of the hottest and quickest growing sales roles over the last decade has been in the field of software sales.

In working with many of these companies, I'm reminded that sales will always be a constant, ever-evolving field; there will always be new technologies and new tools on the market. And it will fall to seasoned sales pros to effectively communicate the benefits of these new tools to the marketplace.

Let's take a look at some tactics indispensable to sales demos with particular focus on software sales pros.

In simplest terms, a sales demo shows how a given solution meets the customer's needs and fits into their current infrastructure, tech enabled growth plans, and customized workflows to increase effectiveness and efficiency.

When I train people on sales demos, I start by making sure there is alignment. I ask, "What is the difference between a product demo and a sales demo?" I want sellers to know that we are not giving "speeds and feeds" of just the functionality or training on how to use the features.

We are demonstrating that we can solve their business needs better than anyone else in the market, including the customer trying to solve it themselves. It is about how we bring sales skills into the sales demo meeting(s) to leverage the tactics and skills we have learned thus far.

Let's further break down the purpose of the sales demo and tie it to the sales tactics we have reviewed already:

- **Prove** we solve their stated (and unstated) needs better than anyone else. Leverage case studies, then question to quantify the pain.

  - Quantify the pain with "commitment" questions to know the business impact they have today.
  - Prove to ALL decision makers that you solve it unlike other players (including them building it).

- **Establish** credibility as an industry/persona expert.

  - Leverage persona, vertical battle cards.
  - Use the G.O.L.D Elevator Pitch Process throughout the sales demo.

- **Overcome** any product objections that might be blockers.

  - Silence is not agreement, so get their perspective.
  - Ensure they know the "must have" and "nice to have" items have been clearly articulated and documented to position yourself as the "must have" solution.

- **Gain/Earn** we are the vendor of choice.

  - Move from "Why change?" to "Why you?" *You* can be the product, the company, and/or yourself as a seller.

- **Set** next steps to move the sales process forward.

  - Ensure you understand their "ability to move forward" (the "A" in "F.A.C.T. Discovery

Process"). This is still part of the "demo" stage, even if the customer asks for pricing. You need to know what they will do with that pricing, how to get it approved, how you can support them, etc.

- o Leverage Right Now Contracts to set next steps and meeting purpose, agenda, and expectations, so the outcomes push the sale forward.
- o Document the main next steps that need to occur, by when, and by whom, so you can have clear alignment with the customer.

I often provide cheat sheets for those who give demos to use. Here are those tested sales demo best practices:

- Keep it simple. No jargon or tech talk unless it is 100% common knowledge. This will help be memorable as a simple, easy-to-use solution that they could easily onboard and adopt. Feature-rich demos generally leave the impression that a product is overly complex. Simplify your demo, so that it highlights a small handful of features, all of which are of high value to the customer. Unless you're demoing for the customer's engineers, focus on what the product will do for the prospect's company, not on how your product functions internally.

- Put a face to your name with video conferences meetings like Zoom. People form an emotional connection with visual engagement, and we should show our personal and helpful side. This is a core asset and competitive differentiator. Use Zoom to share your video and a background to eliminate distraction.

- Always tie your pitch to the customer needs. You're not demonstrating how the product works but rather how the product will help the customer. Every feature you demonstrate must be tied directly to a customer problem or opportunity. What does the feature provide that they cannot do today? Leverage case studies and other customer stories as needed.

- Prepare a script and outline—but don't read from it, or you may come across too robotic. Reading a scripted demonstration sounds dull and lacking in personality. Have an outline of what you intend to cover on a general demo, but figure out how you intend to talk about each point. The talking part of your demo must flow to the rhythm of the product. Ensure you have key questions ready to ask that drive customer commitment to change and with stated urgency to act in the near future.

- Rehearse, rehearse, rehearse.

  o Know what you are going to show, how it plays into the client's needs, what they love, and what causes confusion. You must know the ins and outs of your product, even those that are very technical.
  o Before demonstrating ANYTHING to a customer, know what you're going to say and ask. When you are first starting to deliver demonstrations, it is important to rehearse the entire demonstration beforehand at least five times, so it becomes natural and you use different examples for different customer scenarios.

- Remain flexible. The customer may very well want to take control of the demo. Go along with the customer's suggestions as much as you're able—the last thing you want is to annoy the customer by sticking to the script. Demos are meant to provide the proof to meet the client's needs better than anyone else, so remain flexible to ensure you are hitting the items that they want to see.

- A demo is NOT a product training. Remember that. It should merely reinforce your sales message and prove your sales claims. A good demonstration should reinforce the sales message and prove that your sales claims are true. Make sure your demo shows clearly why your offering is important to the decision makers.

- Don't repeat yourself unless it is a critical pain or a significant unique value that you provide and the customer cares about. Repetition doesn't add credibility—it only makes your product demo lengthy and creates the impression that the product can be cumbersome to use and complicated to understand.

- Record all demos—part of your process of continuous improvement is looking back to see what you can improve on in the future.

- Practice and get feedback on your demonstration and sales skills. The sales tactics most commonly used in demos are:

  - Right Now Contracts—to set up the demo meeting, to start the demo meeting, and at the end of the meeting to set next steps. Here are a few examples:

    - Starting a demo:
      - "As we go through this demo, I am going to challenge you with the (two, four, six) things that (personas) like to see. Please challenge us back, and let's make sure we are both asking questions to make sure we are solving your needs. To make sure we are aligned, let's save the last five minutes

of our hour to review which (two, four, six) things resonated with you, so we know the impact they have on your business and the priority level to move forward. If it does make sense to move forward, then we can discuss what moving forward means, so we are aligned."

- Finishing a Demo:
  - "As I stated at the beginning of our time today, we said we would take the last five minutes and see if we were a fit. To recap, you are struggling with (state pain and the impact). We reviewed how ACME uniquely helps with (recap specific items that we do better than anyone else). With that said, do you think we are a fit?"

    - If no—"Sorry to hear that. Can you tell me where I missed the mark?"

    - If yes—"I agree. So, what would you recommend the next steps be?" (If they do not give you enough detailed specifics, then add to it with things like, "others have also wanted..." or "what I would also recommend would be to...").

o Elevator Pitches—You do not need to give the entire elevator pitch, as they should already have heard it from you. But you can frame what the function does, brag about how people love it, link it to a need, and tie the next steps into what they want to see that helps increase their capabilities. Here is an example:

- "ACME understands and gives you control of your workflows. It is one piece of functionality our customers love. They are so frustrated that their current virtual care platform is clunky and inefficient. It really impacts the patient care they provide, and their patients tell them that. We can help you improve similar issues, but let me make this demo specific to your needs. What areas within your virtual care platform are clunky today that you would love to solve? That way, I will hit the items that are most important to you."

- F.A.C.T. questions. Use the "C" and "T" questions to get the vendor of choice. Then use the "A" to uncover and set up the next steps for the deal to close and the customer to get value from your solution. While all these questions should be asked in demo stage, I admit that the "C" and "T" questions are critical in demos. Always have at least three of each question prepared for demos. You can do it as you enter into a new piece of functionality or as you complete that section of functionality. For example:

  - Starting a piece of functionality:
    - "This next piece of a demo, I want to show you specifics on how we help

with. . . but before I go into too much detail, what are some of the concerns you have today that I should show you to see if we can resolve it for you going forward?"

- "This next part I want to show you is something that most customers love because it helps them overcome the concerns they have with. . . So I know how much detail to go into, how important is that to you today?"

- Ending a piece of functionality:
    - "Now that we showed you this functionality, I am curious to know your thoughts. If you had something like this in place, what would you be able to achieve that you cannot achieve today? On a scale of one to ten, where ten is something you need right away, how would you rate the importance of this functionality?"

Suggested Rep Action Plan

- Reflect back on effective sales demos you have seen. Why did they resonate with you? And what steps can you take to replicate that success in your own approach to demos?

- Ensure you highlight your unique value add in sales demos, so customers can see how you are uniquely different from your competition or what they are doing now (thus avoiding a lost deal to "status quo").

- Prep in advance and score yourself after on how you leveraged key sales tactics in your sales demos. In most sales demos, you should be able to:

  - Give a Right Now Contract
  - Give elevator pitches on the company and the products
  - Ask F.A.C.T. discovery questions—some questions from each letter in F.A.C.T.
  - Leverage customer success stories
  - Recap customer needs at end
  - Set definitive next steps

Suggested Manager Action Plan

- Expose your team to best practices and sales tactics used in sales demos and ensure they have solid examples to draw inspiration from in creating their own demos for customers.

- Help your sellers with the sales tactics by being on calls and helping them ask questions, set a Right Now Contract that saves the last five minutes for reviewing needs, confirming fit and setting next steps.

- Constantly review demos with your reps, as this is the key time where you win the customer over from a technical standpoint. Ensure the features and functions of your tools provide meaningful value for your customers, and make sure they see it and acknowledge it!

BONUS TACTIC 3
—Selling to Enterprise Customers

How does your approach need to change when you're selling to enterprise customers? Do not worry, this is not a trick question.

It's crucial to understand why this is a different domain and challenge altogether. There are two main reasons why enterprise selling is different.

More Complex

- More buyers (approvers, influencers, decision makers, partners, executives)—and they all have opinions and like to express them. So if they cannot reach consensus, then their buying process can significantly slow down, if not come to a pause. If you have multiple "lines of business" that you are working with, then you can see this get even more exponential.

- Higher dollar amount—more users, more dynamic needs, more access—the solution needs to be more complex to handle the multiple needs of a larger organization. Scoping solutions takes a lot more effort for sellers, as does vetting solutions for customers.

- More pressure on discounts, resources, support, and how to sell—you will see more RFPs and procurement teams involved—harder for most reps to differentiate their company and offerings to provide unique value (defined as "we can solve your needs better than anyone else in the market. . . including you, Ms. Customer").

Typically Longer Sales Cycle

- More steps to assess internal needs, evaluate and vet solutions, determine vendor, establish agreements on budget/price, compliance, IT/security, legal, and business terms.

- Be patient with the slowness that the complexity brings, but that does not mean you do not push the business case and priority. Show your grit and desire to help. Be confident that your solution is the best.

- More dollars equals more competition. More side-by-side reviews or "bake offs." It can be harder to prove your unique value. Keep trying to communicate these differences in your communications to all decision makers, influencers, and champions. Even if they are not allowed to take your calls, you can still share thought leadership with them via LinkedIn or other communication avenues. Keep you and your company top of mind!

- Honestly, the politics, bureaucracy, competing priorities, etc., are just tough dynamics. Be aware of them and do your best to manage through them.

Given these differences, what are some of the tactics you need to consider in enterprise selling?

- You must outsell the competition! And that means much higher degrees of sales skills; you need to deliver above and beyond what others will do, so you set the bar that others must rise to. The key sales skills are:

  o You must ensure there is a need, desire, and appetite to change. They cannot stick to status quo—you need a strong "why change" message.

o Be prepared. Do your research. These larger customers are more visible in the market, so you can research the business, the people, their competition, their market share, their goals and initiatives, etc.

o Relationship building at all levels—individual contributor/end user, management, C-level—do not be single-threaded in an account—many sellers just keep connected to the "champion," but go beyond that. Leverage their partners and other vendors who enhance your relationship or offering. Leverage your subject matter experts (solution consultants, sales engineers) and executives to help drive higher level of engagements. Keep in touch with many key individuals throughout the entire sales process (and beyond once you close them to maintain that revenue you worked so hard for. . . and grow it too!).

o Be an expert at asking great questions that have impact and priority for the business to help them achieve their short-term or long-term results (C and T questions from F.A.C.T Discovery Process). Show your customer you know, understand, and have experience solving the problems they have in their environment.

o Help the customers buy—moving forward to get them to commit with action. Help your client build a business case or ensure they know how, and have the materials, to sell you internally. Talk about what other clients in their shoes have done to get the deal across the finish line. Be proactive on raising items and collaborative with your champion to drive items in the correct order and velocity to close the deal as planned.

There are some key tools to help sellers sell and help customers buy:

- o Make sure you stack your toolkit with the capabilities you need to land your target customers, which in many instances will not be unfamiliar to you: account plan, opportunity plan, business personas battlecards, vertical battlecards, product battlecards, decision maker checklist, mutual success plan, executive summaries, structured executive sponsorship program, and leverage referrals.

- o Lots of software to help you too: LinkedIn, DiscoverOrg, Zoom info, Bombora/6Sense to know purchase intent.

Some additional best practices to keep in mind:

- Every contact in the buying process has their own perspective on how to best do the job. . . their job! You need to understand what drives their decisions (both personally and professionally) while helping them solve problems.

- Understanding the industry vertical that your customer is in helps you speak with relevancy and knowledge of their business. It is the best way to establish trust.

- Knowing your products better than anyone else is critical! Not just how they function, but what they solve for your clients. Sharing that value with clients is the art of product positioning.

- As you move through the sales process, you need to help your buyers (a.k.a. Champions) with internal processes and approval steps that drive the deal to close.

- Leveraging executives in the sales process is powerful when done correctly. Beyond joining a call, an executive sponsorship program aligns executive to executive to overcome obstacles and push the deal to close. Commit to the process!

The "5 Questions Checklist" we reviewed before is something I developed years ago for executives to ask their reps to ensure that these large, committed deals would close. I quickly realized that it was an even better tool for reps to use to plan their next meeting, ensure they are on top of each deal, and achieve the success they wanted. Those reps that were disciplined in these questions sold a lot more!

As we reviewed in our previous chapter on gaining commitment, for a salesperson to close a deal, they need to know the answers to these five questions. The same applied with selling to any Enterprise level deal. You need to break these items down in detail and think how it impacts the entire organization:

1. What's the "why" of this deal from the client perspective? What is their compelling event, pain, need, reason for buying? Make sure the need is not surface level.

2. How have you uniquely positioned yourself to solve that client's needs better than anyone else? Based on the needs identified, have you communicated value that others cannot provide?

3. Where are you in winning this deal? Listen for buying signals as well as the potential pitfalls. How is the customer working with you compared to your

competition? Sell smarter by helping your customer build the business case, ROI, proof of concept, success criteria, etc.

4. What are the next steps to get to the close? Listen for the next steps the customer is taking. The more actions the client can take in the process, the better. Overlay your active involvement with executive summaries and mutual success plans to keep a timeline and mutual commitment.

5. How connected are you to all buyers? It is not just the business/department level decision maker you need to get commitment from. Ensure that you are working with the economic, legal, IT/security, or exec committee as well to get their approval and commitment to move forward. It can take winning the trust of a variety of decision makers to ultimately close a sale; keep in mind a checklist of all the relevant decision makers who may be in the mix.

Finally, don't underestimate the importance of an executive sponsor for your sale—someone empowered to cut through the red tape and get your pitch over the finish line past all these decision makers. It is an executive at your company who has power to make commitments and get comments from executives at your customer.

Executive Sponsorship Dos & Don'ts

- **DO:** Meet frequently with the rep to understand the status of the deal, positioning, and the next steps (by leveraging the sales process). If you are a rep, then take the ownership of this as well to help your executive.

- **DO:** Take an active role in key client meetings. Develop relationships with business sponsors and involved executives and negotiate business terms to close. Reps need to help ensure that calendars align and activities are achieved.

- **DO:** Minimize "dead spots" and "stalls"—think creatively about alternative paths to solve the client needs. As you give, try to get something back from the customer.

- **DO:** Coach the rep constructively by debriefing after client interactions and thinking about what could have been done better—do this by asking questions. Explain the "why" and demonstrate the "how." Reps, you can ask for this along the way too, before meetings and/or after meetings.

- **DO:** Provide status updates to exec team as/when needed. Bring in lessons learned, customer feedback, competitive intelligence, etc.

- **DO:** Identify resources from other departments that are needed (product/ops/engineering) and remove hurdles.

- **DON'T:** Encourage the rep to take a passive position by doing their job for them.

- **DON'T:** Think that you must go it alone—leverage the legal, product, services, and finance teams to help.

- **DON'T:** Shortcut the sales process—the rep still needs to maintain accurate and up-to-date records, so that we have visibility into the pipeline and stages.

- **DON'T:** Exclude the rep's manager from updates and feedback.

Suggested Rep Action Plan

- Write out a few key differences with enterprise sellers and others you may have worked with. Challenge yourself to think through how your approach needs to be modified in working with them.

- Spend more time researching contacts, customer news (e.g., an earnings release), and the locations/subsidiaries to develop a detailed plan of attack for the opportunity at hand. This shows you are aligned with their business, acting as a business partner and ensuring you have their best interest at heart!

Suggested Manager Action Plan

- Leverage your role and other executives to be actively involved with these enterprise accounts. We need multiple people from our company to have relationships and developed rapport with the multiple people at the customer level.

- Ensure your executive team is aware of and being held accountable to do their part. Are they just joining a meeting or being an executive sponsor as outlined? Help them along the way with reminders, providing support and information. Ensure there is alignment.

- Coach executives on your sales process and sales tactics, so they are aware of what they are and how to best use them.

- Guide them on how to best work with your rep. You know the way they operate best, as well as their strengths and weaknesses. Bridge the gaps as needed.

BONUS TACTIC #4
—How to Rock a Tradeshow

There are a lot of tradeshows that we all attend, so we need to know how to prepare and execute at tradeshows to maximize engagement! There is a lot involved in making a tradeshow successful. And it's at no small price; it is normally a significant investment, too. In addition, it takes many resources to plan, attend, and follow up.

We need to track the results to ensure we are getting the return on invested dollars and effort. Let's break down these pieces in digestible chunks, so we know how to plan for and achieve the right business results.

Determine the Right Tradeshows to Attend

There are many tradeshows to attend out there, and it is easier than ever to explore the right ones for your team.

Many tradeshows focus on industry events (e.g., International Legal Technology Association), company events (e.g., Annual User Conference), or themes (e.g., Women in Leadership). These events can be national or regional. They can be large tradeshows for anyone to attend or smaller summits by invite only. You can be the host, a sponsor, or an individual attendee.

So, how do we know which tradeshows we want to attend or sponsor?

The easy answer is that you attend the tradeshow that yields the best results. The hard part is defining the expected results and how you will get there. Most common reasons for attending a tradeshow are:

- New buyer acquisition
- Building name recognition/market awareness
- Defending the name you built, especially in key industry or vertical segments
- Supporting key buyers, industries, or topics that are important for the company
- Keeping connected with current buyers
- Trying to advance the sales process for open opportunities

Often, people want to achieve results in every area. This kind of spreading around of limited attention and resources is rarely very successful. While there is definitive overlap between these areas, focus is the key here—as in many parts of life. We need to balance the level of resources (money, time, and people) with the level of effort (time can only be spent on one item at any given time).

Balance these items to determine the reason you want to attend each tradeshow. To best illustrate the point, we will review what is needed as a paid sponsor who is trying to achieve:

- New lead development with unknown or untouched prospects
- Close current opportunities with prospects that will be in attendance
- Connection with current buyer base to show appreciation, provide support, and hopefully leverage to provide recommendations to prospects

What to Do in Advance of the Tradeshow

There is a lot to do before a tradeshow to make sure marketing and sales are aligned.

Marketing teams tend to have an annual marketing plan to look at their budget for determining where they want to spend money and how. They will have budgets specifically for tradeshows and probably have an Excel file somewhere to track the event, date, location, resources needed (e.g., business unit or attendee names), level of sponsorship to see the cost and level of involvement (e.g., booth size, speaking/panel, meals/event sponsorship, etc.), booth set up and configuration, and collateral needs (e.g., print outs for booth, website, presentations, back of hotel keys, elevator wraps, and the always needed booth "giveaways").

There should be a detail pre-event meeting where Sales and Marketing work with all parties involved to ensure:

- Goal of the event and agreement on event targets

- Event logistics—timing, data, location, schedule (i.e. booth management), booth set up, speaking events, lead tracking process

- Pre-meeting marketing and messaging—social, previous year attendee list, this year attendee list, collateral to be provided, next meeting with actions to take by role and date

- Marketing prep for the meeting—message and ask for each reach out message

  o Look at local customers or opportunities (sales should get the list in advance and come to the meeting with this detail, so actions on how to attack are discussed)

  o Reach out to attendee list

- Next steps—specific actions by role with timing

  o Set targets to get the team moving

    ▪ Pre-event reach outs and messaging
    ▪ Pre-event calendar invites for customers, prospects, and in motion live deals

After you have these items for setting up the show, then it is about executing the show.

As a seller, you need to know the level of access you get to the attendees, setting up booths, meeting rooms, conference rooms, demo rooms, or establishing an additional event to draw in customers (e.g., renting out a restaurant). Reps need to ensure they have tracking and metrics built into their process, typically with a campaign code, so they can see the results from the time and effort given.

If marketing has access to attendees in advance, then sales needs to craft and communicate to them before the tradeshow occurs.

Last note for pre-event planning: Be creative with these events. It's not always easy, especially in our current era of so many events shifting to virtual environments, but you must consider that your events and tradeshows today aren't just competing with other tradeshows—they are also competing with all of the other demands on people's attention and eyeballs.

While substance is always first and foremost, it's also essential to consider how to inject excitement and storytelling into the buyer engagements. Some might have the pocketbooks to shell out for a big celebrity/speaker name or large giveaway to help attract attention. Otherwise you may need to get a little more creative with the resources that you do have.

This is especially true in the big events where you need to create buzz and excitement. I have seen wonderful examples where sponsors of an event have created buyer awards where they have announced winners and provided buyer accolades. They hyped it up both before and during the event.

And just as crucial, they followed through with it post event and continued to have it each year where it grew in awareness, stature, and desire to win across prospects or buyers.

Many salespeople just show up to events. No plan, no agenda, no targets. They are not prepared or organized. You need to know the prospects who will be attending—either new or those attending where there are current opportunities open that you are trying to close.

You also need to know what current buyers will be attending the tradeshow, so you can ensure they are happy and can leverage those who are fans.

Planning this in advance is critical. If this is a major show, then four to eight weeks in advance is normal for sales to get involved. It takes time to get the layout of the details and marketing put together. It also gives you time to pre-establish meetings before the event starts. Ensure that meetings, demos, meals, or other activities with prospects or clients are established and accepted to maximize results.

What to Do When Working the Booth at a Tradeshow

So many times, I see people at tradeshows looking around. They think of it more like a party than a distraction from their "selling time." To make the most of these types of events, everyone must be willing to execute and drive the success. If that is not your mentality, then you should not attend these events. Here are some critical things to do at the tradeshow:

- Accountability meetings are critical. Most people just show up, and once the booth is set up, they let the fun times begin. There is a lot to do in advance of your first visitor in the exhibit hall:

  o Get everyone at the booth in advance to see layout, materials, giveaways, lead tracking process, and key focus points. Practice pitches (yes—live role playing for all). This is also a great time to test out any technology for demonstration, lead tracking, or special booth technology (e.g., badge scanner).

  o Ensure everyone knows the schedules for booth duty, client meetings, key vendor presentations, meals, and extra events. Depending on the scale of the tradeshow and the quantity of people in attendance, you might assign out specific functions for each person.

    ▪ One person to take pictures of event space, speakers, and events and post it on social media, your LinkedIn company page, and the event social media outlets.
    ▪ One person to follow up with current buyers that are in attendance. Invite them to the booth and make them feel your appreciation for their business.
    ▪ One person as the overall coordinator to align schedules and management of the event. This could include working with channel partners, event sponsors, or strategic relationships as needed. They can

also ensure all leads are scanned and assigned correctly.

- o Get a lay of the land. Look to see who else is there and any competition you have. See if you can get their materials and see their layout, so you know how to position yourself in a more unique fashion where others won't be vying with you for attention.

- Have your three-to-five-second saying to get them intrigued as they walk by—what is easy to say, easy to understand, and engaging (funny, valuable, makes them think "OK, who are you?"). And the more unique you are, the more you will stand out. Ultimately, I want a "passerby" to look me in the eye and choose to engage with me. If I want that to happen, I have to make it happen. I would say some very random items just to be different and spark them to reply to me that is not the usual, "Hi, how are you?" or "Want to win an iPad?" I would rotate these examples below throughout the event so when people walk by a second or third time, I am still unique:

  - o Would you like my autograph, too?
  - o Can you sign my kids' yearbook?
  - o Heads or tails? (and flip a coin and have them come look)
  - o Beer or wine? (tie it to an event you are doing)
  - o Hawaii or Jamaica?
  - o Or if you are giving a prize like an Apple Watch then "Fitbit or Apple Watch?"
  - o Internal or External. I used that at a conference where I was selling internal communication software. I would say "internal or external" and people would look at me confused. JACKPOT. They looked at me so I

stepped toward them and asked, "Internal or external communication—what is more important?" It was a great way to engage people and draw them into the booth and learn more about our solutions.

- Once you have them engaging with you and making eye contact, then you have one to two minutes. So be ready! Have a strong elevator pitch on what you do, along with great questions teed up to engage them and kick off the conversation—something like, "I know you are here for probably a few reasons, but what are the top three things you hope to get out of this conference?" If they do not mention a solution that your team offers, then ask them point blank, "So would having a solution that does ABC (value points that mirror your elevator pitch) be of importance for your business? And are you free to set up time later today where we can sit down and talk in more detail... maybe even bring a team member of yours with you?"

- If they want to learn more, try to do it then or set up time to schedule them to come back for a demo (and set the stage with a little discovery or unique value now). Determine the best course of action based on the scenario, but be aggressive.

  o People attend these sessions to learn, so providing a demo or reviewing your solution at the same time as the speaking session might be more valuable to your prospect. Do not assume that only during the exhibition hall time is when they will want to see more. ASK THEM!

  o Ensure the right team is there. Often people attend tradeshows with a colleague, so ensure you have all the right decision makers or decision influencers there.

- Document your client interactions, so you know the people, companies, and their needs. Then you can quickly track and take action. Do not wait or just mark all conversations the same in your follow-up. You need to know some people in particular:

  o Attendees—get them into a marketing automation system or "nurture" program.
  o Attended the booth and showed minor interest (e.g., took some collateral, dropped a business card in the fishbowl to win a prize, or "window shopped" to see who you are)—get them part of the SDR follow-up. Have an email to them THE SAME DAY they stopped by your booth.
  o Wanted a demo—set it up or have the follow-up go out that day to set it up. Get it on the calendar!
  o Received a demo—hopefully you have identified where they are in the buying process and started to work that deal with a demo showing your unique value proposition.

- Set follow-up meetings right then and get them on the calendar before the tradeshow is over. Time is of the essence! In the invite, remind them (and yourself) of what you talked about as your solution, how it ties to their need, and what the next step is, so they do not forget you among all the other vendors. Not to mention, you will have the meeting established while every other seller is calling just to get them on the phone for the next two weeks. Be smarter and more proactive than your competition!

- If you have a different event space for meetings or demos, have a schedule for people and buyer alignment. Book as much of this before the event as possible and ensure you proactively communicate to attendees in advance with a reminder email the day before with location, local contact, and the reason they need to attend (a.k.a. the "Right Now Contract") to show the value they will get from the meeting.

- If you have buyers who will be in attendance, have them come by the booth for a visit (or a thank you gift) as they can talk to prospective clients for you. If you have good rapport with your client, I would even ask them to attend specific events like the booth, dinner with a prospective client, or even a client demo. Leverage these client testimonials, especially at tradeshows when people are face-to-face. At the very least, reach out and meet them for breakfast or lunch at the event, so you can get face time, have a check in, and show them a little love.

- For those that understand the value and have the ability to whiteboard key sales messages, this tip will change your tradeshow interactions. Keep a stack of 8X5 notepads with you that has your company/product logo(s) in the header section and then all your contact information in the footer. Think about it. We all give our business cards, but rarely do we know what we talked about with that person. Or we have marketing materials that are generic, not tailored to me. When people engage you in a conversation and you can provide them specifics via whiteboarding, that is the leave behind that matters and provides action. In fact, I tend to have one pen with multiple color options, so I can frame things in black, some pain in red, and next steps in blue.

So, here is one story that I have to share on this topic. I was working with a company and convinced them that they needed to have more buyer engagement added to these tradeshows. They wanted prospective clients to see how much they care about their current clients.

They knew this was a strength of theirs and believed they were different than any other company out there. So, they created awards to celebrate their buyer base. The tradeshow lasted two days and had a large networking break in the vendor hall in the AM and PM agendas of both days. So, they created four awards and invited their buyers.

They purchased plaques and engraved the awards for the company and the person. When the buyer came by, they would yell out something to the effect of, "Excuse me, everybody. Can I get your attention please? At Quick Hit Sales T.I.P.S. we value our buyers and are excited to announce a buyer award to [person] from [company] for [award type]. Everyone please give [person] a round of applause."

And can you guess what happened from there? Come on, think bigger than that! Everyone starts clapping and cheering. The booths next door do not want to be rude, so they clap too.

As you give the award, a teammate takes a picture of it. It gets posted on social media and tags the event, your excited buyer, and their company. You start to become the buzz. Especially as you do this for each of your awards (buyer insight award, best buyer feedback award, best contributor, highest active user, best administrator, etc.).

And, yes, you can make this award monthly and quarterly to leverage this tactic outside of tradeshows. Not only was the buyer happy and most likely going to remain a buyer for a long time, but you got others to be inspired, created buzz for free, and engaged clients in ways that no one else at the tradeshow did.

Sales Manager (and Marketing) Execution Tip

- Establish the expectations needed with your sales team in advance. You must think through the executional aspects and ensure the sales team is prepared in advance. Items like:

  o How you want them to set meetings up in advance of the tradeshow.
  o The quantity of meetings you want set up in advance.
  o How they will support seller open deals or buyers that will not be attending.
  o How you expect them to handle events, leads, tracking, or even expenses.

- Post tradeshow debrief to review what worked well, what didn't work well, how we are following up, and prioritizing leads versus those more meaningful discussions.

- And the most important piece of it all, track your results! You need to know the return you are getting for the time, energy, and dollars spent. It is not just the hard costs with the event (including travel and meals) but also the opportunity cost for sellers not calling on other buyers or working open deals.

Sales Ops: Many times sales ops are not part of the process for tradeshows. There are critical items that are needed to ensure the people, process, and systems connect fluidly, so there is proper execution. Items may include:

- Campaign code tracks from Marketing Automation Platform (MAP) into lead tracking process into salesforce automation systems (CRM like Salesforce.com).

- Helping sales leadership determine how to best staff the show.

- Ensure the tracking and reinforcement items are established in advance. Make sure reports align and that the communication patterns from sellers to executives are clear.

Suggested Rep Action Plan

- Write out a list of upcoming tradeshows to target. Where do you see the most opportunity? How do you need to modify your approach given the crowd?

- Prepare for the tradeshow in advance by knowing the types of attendees and how you can be relevant to their needs.

- Practice your tactics to gain their attention. Have a strong elevator pitch, a quick follow-up process, and a plan to get them to see your solution as much as possible while at the event.

Suggested Manager Action Plan

- Give "stretch opportunities" to members of your team to attend tradeshows; seek out opportunities for them to actively learn on the job.

- Do not let them attend tradeshows unless they have certain numbers of customer meetings that are already on the calendar.

- Ensure your reps take it seriously, and not just as a party.

BONUS TACTIC # 5
—Always Be Coached

The ABCs of selling is not "always be closing" but rather "always be coached." I put this chapter at the end because if you've read this much of the book, then my assumption is your ego is not big enough where you don't want to improve. Making conscious improvements to your sales skills and utilizing new tactics is not easy.

There is no shame in being coached and the most successful professionals tend to get coached often and by multiple people. The 2022 Los Angeles Dodgers have ten different coaches under their manager Dave Roberts. There are hitting coaches, pitching coaches, a first base coach, a third base coach, bullpen coaches, and multiple assistant coaches. There is even a game planning and communication coach. Even the Los Angeles Lakers have nine coaches. These players are the most elite athletes, and some make some of the biggest paydays of all time.

So, sellers must have coaches as well. They can be your manager, an executive, a peer, a customer, and even yourself (if you are honest with yourself). But the secret here is to make conscious efforts on how you execute your sales skills. Are you like Michael Jordan who practices until he cannot do it wrong in the game? His coach guides him, but his effort and focus on improving a very specific part of his game is one item that makes him the elite legend that Michael Jordan is to the game of basketball.

So, sellers, here is my challenge to you. I want you to leverage multiple coaches in your sales career to help you improve upon skills that you need to improve upon as well as ensure you continue to execute flawlessly on the skills you are great at. Go back to the beginning of this book and look at all the sales skills that were listed. Determine for yourself where you need to improve and who can help you improve in that area. Then make it happen with targeted coaching and conscious efforts on where you can improve. Go into every training or team meeting with the thought of, "How can I leave here better than when I walked in?" Read sales books like this one. Listen to sales podcasts. Join LinkedIn sales groups. There are many ways you can improve your skill; you must make it happen for yourself.

One of the best ways to coach yourself is to evaluate a sales call. If you're doing it over the phone, then record it (via system or with your own cell phone). As you review your call or if you review it with your manager/coach, ask yourself:

- What specific skill or two am I evaluating?

- What did I do right with that skill that I want to continue to do?

- What did I want to improve with that skill?

- Set an action plan of:

  o What will you do to improve? Get specific with the details and how you plan to improve.
  o When/how often you will do it?
  o When do I want to review my progress and evaluate my performance again?

I have worked with many reps on this, and the more specific they are, the better. Here is an example of how a rep I coached evaluated their ability to perform the F.A.C.T. Discovery Process. For background, she was a younger seller with only a few years of sales experience. She was concerned she would always be a "C player," and she hated that. She was not used to being "average."

She was always successful and knew she did not have all the answers. She wanted to learn from everyone and make changes in her results ASAP. She followed up her action plan with me as follows:

. . .

Scott, thank you for your time coaching me today. I appreciate the honesty, push, and role-playing support you gave, so I can see some live examples. Here is my action plan to work on F.A.C.T:

- I am good at asking "F" questions. I need to keep doing that, so I can understand their current environment, the systems they use, and the teams involved with using and supporting that system. Asking in all those areas really frames the needs they have and what they want to see in a demo.

- I need to work on "C" questions and "T" questions a lot. I plan to do this by:

  o Getting over my fear of not knowing the answer or asking my customer hard questions about the business impact their current environment is having on them.
  o I am going to get three "C" and three "T" questions prepared for each demo meeting. I will write them out first, practice them out loud at least three times, and ensure that I get the answer that

    ▪ Gives me ways they want to change ("C" questions)
    ▪ Gives me the priority to act on that change ("T" questions)

o   I am going to take detailed notes on the answers to these questions and recap them in the last five minutes, so the client knows I heard them and understand their needs. I will use that to drive next steps.

I am going to be practicing this starting tonight and will incorporate this into my demos starting tomorrow. I feel comfortable with the questions we practiced today, so I know what I want to do. . . I just need to do it! I will record both calls tomorrow and review them myself, so I can get better at self-evaluation. I will then make any adjustments and will send you my demo recording from the demos I have on Friday. I will make notes when I ask the questions, so you do not have to listen to the entire call. We can review that in our next 1:1.

Let me know if you think I am missing anything.

. . .

I appreciate the level of detail she gave. But I really loved the action she took. She did exactly what she said she would do. She even went a step further and had a peer review her calls asking for them to only focus in on her questions. She was delighted to get the feedback and hear that the rep took something from her. They instantly became accountability partners and started working with each other once a week. She turned her coaching with me into coaching herself and getting coached from her peer.

As our coaching progressed, she got a rhythm down. She did not want to try to fix everything all at once. Every month, she took two new skills she wanted to work on to improve. Maybe she was awful at those skills or maybe she was good but wanted to be better. She developed a plan each month that took her about twenty to thirty minutes. She would email it to me, her manager, and her accountability partners. (She rotated them based on their ability to help her. They were peers, cross functional teams, and some executive coaches too.) Within six months, she was leading her team. Within a year, she was consistently in the top five reps of her sales team of roughly sixty quota carrying reps.

While she loved achieving the results, she was glad that she was able to overcome obstacles and not let herself be the reason for the lack of success. She challenged herself and won. She helped her team and they won too (her accountability peers are also in the top five).

I have coached many others like her. I love hearing about their success and seeing their progress. I love the grit and lack of egos! I love that many people I coach leverage their team to improve, so everybody wins.

Hopefully this book helped you in that process. It was intentional that we finished every chapter with a suggested rep action plan and a manager coaching plan to help you drive adoption and fluidity in the tactic and enhance your results to achieve more than you have in the past.

Suggested Rep Action Plan

- Reflect on coaches you've had in your life, whether in the workplace or on the playing field. What skills did they pass on and how can you effectively coach and inspire those around you?

- Determine three coaches you want to have in your current role. They can be managers, executives, peers, consultants, coaches, etc. Write down what you want from them, so you can be specific in your requests. Then ask them to be your coaches and set up recurring times to meet with them.

- Practice self-awareness and self-assessment. You are the only one who will read every email and hear every call you have. Practice self-evaluation, so you can coach yourself!

Suggested Manager Action Plan

- Hold yourself accountable for your skills in coaching your team, not simply giving orders. What can you do to climb down into the trenches with them, while still giving them room to succeed and face challenges with autonomy?

- Coach daily! You can coach a rep to ensure they are prepared for a meeting. You can coach a rep from a meeting you were in and part of. You can coach reps post a meeting to see how the meeting went, what occurred, and what were the next steps to make sure it matched the desired outcome.

Conclusion

And there you have it!

Part of the thrill of sales is never fully knowing what to expect when you walk into any room. You can't prepare or over-engineer for each and every eventuality. Throughout my career, I've learned that virtually any client can throw you a curveball when you least expect it.

I have also learned that you can be prepared for most curveballs if you are focused and diligent. You can outsell your competition and develop wonderful customer relationships!

By preparing yourself with this full roster of tactics, you'll expand the capabilities in your toolkit and be able to walk into any room prepared to take on any challenge.

Sales is a stimulating journey of a career—continually offering new opportunities to learn, grow, and problem solve. That's what has kept me engaged, and I trust you'll find no shortage of exciting challenges at any level or phase in your own career journey.

I finish most of my emails and trainings with the phrase "Good Selling." I think it is unique, but it also sends a message. . . you have to purposefully be good. It takes practice, diligence, and ideas that you can morph into your style, words, and tonality.

I hope you took something from each chapter and can leverage these tactics and skills in your sales career. Use the scripts or take the concepts and make them your own! Work on a tactic for a week or two. . . or three or four if you need to. Use the suggested rep action plans. Ask for help from peers or social networks. Make your sales career the most fun and lucrative career you have ever had!

With that. . . I wish you GOOD SELLING!

Please look for more Quick Hit Sales T.I.P.S. and share your thoughts on our website of www.QuickHitSalesTips.com or our LinkedIn page: https://www.linkedin.com/company/quick-hit-sales-tips/

QuickHitSalesTips.com